JENNIE LOW'S
CHOPSTICKS, CLEAVER, AND WOK

HOMESTYLE CHINESE COOKING

CHRONICLE BOOKS

SAN FRANCISCO

DEDICATION

This book is dedicated to all my friends and students, past and present, who have been inspirational in its creation. Their continual requests for a compilation of my recipes, their repeated assurances as to the clarity of the directions, and their unwavering support of my project have resulted in *Chopsticks, Cleaver, and Wok*. To each of them, my gratitude.

A special thanks to Doong Tien and Lauan Garnjost for their work on the manuscript.

To my husband, John, whose talents and abilities were of great help, and to our very own Cincy and Denise, who assisted me in my cooking classes, I express my deep and lasting appreciation.

Library of Congress Cataloging-in-Publication Data:
Low, Jennie, 1940–
Chopsticks, cleaver, and wok: homestyle Chinese cooking.
p. cm.
Includes index.
ISBN 0-8118-1666-4 (pbk.)
1. Cookery, Chinese. I. Title.
TX724.5.C5L6512 1997
641.5951—dc21   96-51125
CIP

Printed in the United States of America.

Cover photograph: Zeva Oelbaum
Cover design: Elizabeth Van Itallie
Book design: Thomas Ingalls + Associates
Composition: On Line Typography

Distributed in Canada by Raincoast Books
8680 Cambie Street
Vancouver, B.C. V6P 6M9

10 9 8 7 6 5 4 3 2 1

Chronicle Books
85 Second Street
San Francisco, California 94105

Web Site: www.chronbooks.com

TABLE OF CONTENTS

PREFACE 4

GENERAL INFORMATION 5

Wok Mei 6

Chopsticks 7

Cooking Utensils 8

Cooking Methods 11

Cutting Techniques 14

Ingredients Used in Chinese Cooking 19

How to Plan a Chinese Menu 32

The Chinese Tea Lunch 32

APPETIZERS 35

SOUPS 49

POULTRY 61

MEAT 87

FISH AND SHELLFISH 105

VEGETABLES 123

CLAY-POT, SIZZLING-PLATTER, AND FIREPOT DISHES 135

NOODLES, WON TONS, AND RICE 143

INDEX 158

Each time I begin teaching a new cooking class, all the students seem to be asking me the same question: "Can I *learn* to cook Chinese food?" I always tell them this story.

Twenty-eight years ago, I arrived in the United States from Hong Kong. I spoke little English. Worse yet, I did not even know how to cook a pot of rice. My uncle, with whom I lived, was a master chef at a local restaurant. Every Wednesday, his day off, he prepared marvelous foods at home for the family. He would say to me, "Watch now, so that you will know how to cook this yourself one day." But I was young and carefree and didn't listen. We would all sit down, eat the delicious dinner, and then wash the dishes. And after the meal my uncle would always exclaim, "Oh, Jennie. How will you ever learn how to cook?"

Then one day I married, and my husband was a man who enjoyed his Chinese food—food the way his mother cooked it. What was I to do? My uncle was no longer alive to teach me. So I asked Auntie, "How do you cook fish heads like my husband's mother does?" And she answered, "Ask his mother." But of course I couldn't do that. So Auntie told me, "Chop the fish, add a sprinkle of this, a sprinkle of that, and you have it."

I learned to cook just that way—the sprinkle way. And if a dish was too salty or too spicy, then the next time I sprinkled in a little less of this, a little more of that. By using this method, I have mastered more than two hundred recipes, many of which I am sharing with you in these pages. Each recipe has been developed by cooking it first in my customary manner, then fixing it a second time while painstakingly recording measurements for each ingredient. In this way the unique flavor of the dish has been preserved so that it can be duplicated by you.

Most of these recipes cannot be classified into any particular "regional style," such as Cantonese or Hunanese. During years of cooking at home and teaching my classes, I have transformed many dishes that were basically Cantonese into something quite different, to suit the tastes of my family, my students, and myself. Perhaps a dish that was at one time classically Cantonese is now more akin to the Peking or Szechuan kitchen. Each recipe carries two names, however, one in English and one in Cantonese, the Chinese dialect most widely spoken in the United States.

If you follow my recipes faithfully, I am confident that you too will become an expert at Chinese cooking. And perhaps you will develop your very own "sprinkle" system.

General Information

WOK MEI

All Chinese cooks strive for *wok mei*, literally, "good flavor." But in its fuller sense the phrase describes the satisfaction of each of the five senses, sight, smell, taste, texture, and temperature, imparted by a well-prepared dish. *"Ho wok mei"* is the ultimate compliment that one can give a Chinese cook.

To achieve *wok mei*, a culinary creation must be pleasing to the eye. The inclusion of bright-green pepper slices to a basically red sweet-and-sour dish contributes to the *wok mei* by adding a contrasting color. The Chinese cook may arrive at the same effect in other dishes with generous amounts of coriander (Chinese parsley).

The *heung*, or "aroma," of a dish also contributes to *wok mei*. Every preparation should release its own distinctive, pleasing aroma, for food that smells good will taste good. Here are the secret steps for giving all your Chinese stir-fry dishes that special *heung*. First, always heat the wok until it smokes. Add the cooking oil by pouring it into the wok in a circular motion around the lip. If you have a one-handled wok, you can rotate it briefly to coat the cooking surface. If you are using a two-handled wok, scoop the oil up the sides with the spatula. The heat of the wok will heat the oil almost instantly. Add the garlic and ginger, if called for in the recipe. Allow these to sizzle a little before you add your main ingredients. Temperature control is critical! The wok should not be so hot it burns the food; far worse is too little heat. A "feel" for the correct temperature will come with experience.

Taste is, of course, of primary importance to any culinary pursuit. The seasoning amounts in my recipes are moderate, to suit the majority of people. By varying measurements to please yourself and your guests, you may fashion your own *wok mei*.

The fourth component of good *wok mei* is texture. All foods have their own natural texture, and it must be preserved in the cooking process. For example, meat should come out firm yet tender, while broccoli, celery, and carrots should add crispness to a dish. Bean cake is ideally soft but dense, and noodles are best when the outside is just beginning to soften and the inside is still slightly hard. The texture of ingredients is retained by strict attention to the temperature of the pan and to cooking time. Most vegetables are ready in just a few minutes when cooked over high heat, for instance.

Finally, *wok mei* demands the serving of food at its proper temperature. Hot foods should be served *hot*, cold foods should be served *cold*, and stir-fry dishes should be served immediately after turning out of the wok.

This is my humble attempt to describe the intangible *wok mei*. Some cooks achieve it effortlessly with everything they cook, even something as simple as a fried egg. Others strive for years without ever achieving it. May every dish you serve receive a *"ho wok mei"* from your guests.

CHOPSTICKS

The Chinese use chopsticks as easily and as naturally as Europeans use forks. They are like an extension of a man's fingers, practical adaptations that evolved from the days when man indeed ate with his fingers.

There are different styles of chopsticks. The Chinese variety is blunt on the "eating end," while the Japanese prefer those with pointed tips. There are even short lengths for children to use. Chopsticks are made of many materials—ivory, plastic, silver, and even jade—but the most common ones are of wood or bamboo. For everyday use, wood, bamboo, or ivory is best. Plastic chopsticks are not satisfactory, since they tend to warp after repeated immersion in hot washing water.

All Chinese food is prepared so that it may be easily handled with chopsticks. In fact, many older-generation Chinese households have no forks at all. Fingers really have to work in order to use these implements adeptly, however, and our fingers have become lazy from eating with forks. Practice is the key to success with these centuries-old tools.

Even rice poses no problem with chopsticks, if you eat it from a bowl as the Chinese do. The rice bowl is held close to the mouth and the rice is "shoveled" in with the sticks. Such a method would be frowned on in an elegant French restaurant, but is perfectly acceptable when eating Chinese food. Incidentally, "rice plates," in which stir-fried or braised foods are spooned over rice mounded on a dish, are a Western innovation and the Chinese eat them Western style, with a fork.

Chopsticks are used for cooking as well as eating. They are good for serving noodles, retrieving deep-fried foods, beating eggs, and stir-frying. One can even buy extra-long "cooking chopsticks," which make these kitchen tasks even easier.

How to Use Chopsticks

Think of chopsticks as extensions of your fingers that move in a pincer action. Ideally the chopsticks are held along the upper third of their length and certainly no lower than the middle. If held too low, much of the pincer action will be lost. Practice first by picking up large pieces of food such as chunks of celery or meat. You will have achieved mastery when you can pick up a button mushroom that is swimming in slippery oyster sauce.

1. Rest one chopstick in the groove between thumb and forefinger. Notice that the middle finger, along with the others, is curved inward to support the chopstick.

2. With the first chopstick in place, grasp the second between thumb and forefinger, as you would hold a pencil.

3. Now, operate your chopsticks by moving the top stick in an up-and-down motion to meet the lower stick. Keep the bottom stick stationary. All you need at this point is practice.

COOKING UTENSILS

Chinese cooking utensils have evolved over centuries of use into forms best suited to their particular functions. Using them will simplify the preparation of dishes, but you can still cook good Chinese food without them.

Recipes in this book specify a wok, but at first don't hesitate to try a pan you already have in your kitchen. For example, a cast-iron skillet can be used for stir-frying small amounts of vegetables, as it retains heat well. Then, as you become more familiar with Chinese cooking techniques, you may decide you want to purchase a wok and other specialized equipment. (I can almost guarantee that you will find the wok so convenient and efficient that you will begin using it to prepare Western food as well.)

The following information will guide you to the most practical utensils. If possible, shop in an Asian neighborhood for the best buys.

The Wok

The wok is the most important utensil in the Chinese kitchen. Traditionally made of heavy iron or steel and equipped with two handles, this versatile, concave-shaped pan is used for stir-frying, deep-frying, pan-frying, steaming, and stewing. Its ancient design has been adapted for modern use with a metal ring, which the pan sits in on the burner. Even more contemporary are the stainless-steel woks with flat copper bottoms that rest directly on the burner. These usually have a single long handle similar to that on a skillet and are lighter and easier to use than the classic two-handled pan.

There are numerous models of electric woks available, many of them quite satisfactory. I do find, however, that the thermostats on some models will not keep the temperature at the highest heat for the time necessary to complete a dish. Also, if a dish has several steps, it is inconvenient to disconnect the cord in order to wash the wok and then reconnect it for the next step.

Before their first use, stainless-steel, electric, and nonstick woks should be washed and air-dried. Carbon-steel woks must be "seasoned." To do this, add ½ c. oil (this can be oil saved from deep-frying) to the wok and spread it around to coat the inside surface thoroughly. Cook over medium-low heat for 15 minutes, recoating the surface with oil periodically. Discard the oil. Wipe the wok clean with a paper towel, then wash it with soap and water. Dry over medium heat. This oil treatment keeps the wok from rusting and must be done only once. Thereafter, wash the wok as usual. Continue to dry the wok over heat after washing for the first 20 times you use it, to complete the seasoning process by sealing the pores of the iron. After that, the wok may be wiped dry without fear of rusting.

Buy the necessary accessories at the same time you buy your wok. You will need a cover, a spatula, a perforated plate for steaming, and a bamboo-and-wire strainer.

Your success in Chinese cooking will depend in no small measure upon your mastery of cooking with this remarkable utensil. I wish you good luck!

The Spatula

The Chinese spatula is specially designed for stir-frying in the wok. The edge of the spatula bowl is rounded to fit the shape of the pan, and the utensil itself is sturdier overall than the usual American one, to allow stirring and tossing of large quantities of food. Buy a stainless-steel spatula; it will last a lifetime.

The Cleaver

The Chinese cook does many things with a cleaver: minces garlic, peels fresh water chestnuts, cuts vegetables into delicate, fanciful shapes. In the absence of the modern meat grinder, a pair of cleavers put to work simultaneously will achieve the same results. An expert fascinates and entertains children by peeling an apple with this broad-bladed knife, removing the skin in one long continuous strip. In restaurants there is often one person who, because of expertise with the cleaver, does nothing but cut and chop. The products of that labor show a remarkable skill.

The flat side of the cleaver blade has its own invaluable uses. To peel garlic, firmly whack the clove with it and the skin will fall away. Another whack and a few quick chops and the garlic is finely minced. A deft scrape and the flat of the blade transports the minced garlic to a dish. Water chestnuts and sliced ginger can also be efficiently minced after a firm slap with the side of the blade. Even the handle of the cleaver is invaluable. Use the butt end as a pestle to reduce black beans to a paste or to smooth a bean sauce.

At first glance, the cleaver appears quite formidable, and it certainly should be treated with care and respect. However, working with it will quickly convince you of its utility and fine balance. Mastery of this special utensil requires practice, though. A safe, easy way to develop a "feel" for the cleaver is to cut large items like french bread, squash, or watermelon. As you become more proficient, try your hand at cutting carrot sticks and potatoes for french fries, finally progressing to the thin slicing required for fine julienne. The broad, flat blade is an excellent guide for making nice, even slices. Be sure always to work on a firm surface.

To avoid cutting your fingers as they hold the food, curve them under so that the knuckles act as a guide against the blade. As long as you never raise the blade higher than your knuckles, you will not cut yourself. As an additional safeguard, slant the knife slightly away from the holding hand.

To mince meat for a dumpling filling or pork cake, trim off and discard the fat, then cut the meat into 1″ cubes. Chop with the cleaver, gathering and turning the meat often with the blade to assure an even texture. To speed up the job, use a cleaver in each hand, alternating the strokes.

Cleavers are available in various grades of steel. The best all-purpose tool is made of high carbon steel, which takes a good edge and is heavy enough to cut through bones. Stainless-steel cleavers are fine for cutting vegetables but are too thin for heavy-duty chopping.

Cleavers come in weights, usually indicated by numbers. Try to find one that is comfortable for you. The most commonly used sizes are no. 3 and no. 4. Cleavers usually have wooden handles, but one-piece steel styles are also available.

Never put a cleaver in the dishwasher. Wash it by hand and wipe dry immediately to prevent rust. To sharpen, use a hand or electric knife sharpener or whetstone. Lacking these, the edge of a concrete step or the unglazed ridge on the bottom of a ceramic bowl are adequate substitutes.

The Chinese Wire Strainer

This wide, flat wire strainer with a long bamboo handle is very useful for removing deep-fried foods from hot oil or noodles from boiling water. The most common size for home use is 6″ in diameter.

Steamers

You can steam foods in your wok by placing a flat, perforated metal "steam plate" in the bottom. The curved sides of the wok support the steam plate several inches above the boiling water. The food may be placed directly on the steam plate, or as is more often the case, in a shallow dish or pie plate placed on the steam plate. There is also a footed "steam rack," smaller in diameter than the steam plate, which stands on the bottom of the wok and supports the dish of food well above the water level. Both the steam plate and steam rack are quite inexpensive. The steam plate is probably the best choice of the two, since if a hot dish is accidentally dropped during removal from the pot, the food doesn't end up in the steaming water.

You may prefer to buy a traditional bamboo steamer, which is attractive enough to double as a serving tray for the steamed foods. It is especially fun to own one if you regularly serve *deem sum* (either homemade or purchased). The bamboo steamer has the additional asset of allowing more than one layer of food to be steamed simultaneously—just stack a second basket on top of the first. These steamers are placed above hot water in a wok. They must be at least a full 1″ smaller than the diameter of the pan to prevent damage to the sides of the steamers from the heat source. Also, be sure that the steamer lid has a tight fit.

An aluminum steamer has a bottom pan that holds the water, one or two perforated steaming levels, and a cover, all of which fit together in a manner similar to the way a double boiler stacks. Since the unit is self-contained, your wok can be used at the same time for preparing other dishes.

Look for the ingenious two-armed metal pincer utensil designed for removing hot dishes from the steamer. It is especially handy if there is little clearance between the dish rim and side of the steamer. A slight squeeze causes the tool to grasp opposite edges of the dish so that it can be removed safely with one hand.

The Sizzling Platter

Sizzling-platter dishes, also called "iron-plate" or "teppan" dishes, have recently become popular menu items in Chinese restaurants. These dishes are named for the heavy iron platter that is used for serving. The platter is heated to a high temperature, placed on its wooden tray, and delivered to the table. When hot stir-fried food is spooned onto the platter, the sizzle is very dramatic.

The Clay Pot

Clay-pot dishes are the Oriental version of the American casserole. The main difference is that they are cooked on top of the stove rather than in the oven. Clay pots come with lids and either single or double handles. The interior of the pot is glazed, while the exterior is unglazed. The design assures good retention of heat, so that even if dinner is delayed, the food stays piping hot.

COOKING METHODS

The majority of Chinese cooking methods are common to the Western kitchen. Even stir-frying, which at first might seem quite exotic, is basically a sautéing technique. The primary concern in China has always been the conservation of fuel. Because of this, home cooking has traditionally been of the stove-top variety, using the techniques of stir-frying, pan-frying, deep-frying, steaming, and stewing. Roasting, which requires more heat and therefore considerably more fuel, is left to commercial establishments with specially designed ovens. You will find few recipes here that call for the use of an oven.

    The most essential element of Chinese cooking, and sometimes the most difficult to accomplish, is to have everything you are going to use close at hand. This is especially important when stir-frying, as there is no time to stop in the middle of a recipe to stir up a slurry of cornstarch and water or chop a bell pepper. If you do stop, the dish will overcook. Plan ahead!

    I am often asked what type of stove, gas or electric, is best for Chinese cooking. I find that I have more control of the heat when using a gas flame, so that is my preference. Electricity is just as satisfactory for those accustomed to working with it, however.

Stir-Frying

Stir-frying is the cooking method most often used in the Chinese kitchen. Essentially it is cooking food in a small amount of oil over high heat, stirring constantly so the food is never in contact with the cooking surface long enough to burn. Vegetables retain their natural color and texture, and meats, poultry, and seafood come out tender and juicy.

The Chinese word for stir-frying is *chow;* when you see it used as a prefix on a Chinese menu, you will know the dish is stir-fried. Thus, *chow mein* means stir-fried noodles, *chow fon* is stir-fried rice, *chow fun* is stir-fried rice noodles, and *chow don* is stir-fried eggs.

The first secret to successful stir-frying is to preheat the wok until it begins to smoke. Only then should you add the oil (*never* add oil to a cold wok), pouring it in a circular motion along the lip of the pan. The heat of the wok will heat the oil almost instantly. If the recipe calls for garlic and ginger, add them now and allow them to sizzle about 30 seconds to flavor the oil. Then add your main ingredients and stir constantly with a spatula until done. Vegetables require only about 1 to 2 minutes, while fish, meat, and seafoods cook in about 2 to 3 minutes. Temperature control is critical, but a "feel" for the correct heat intensity will come with experience.

The basic technique of a simple stir-fry dish is to cook the vegetables first and set them aside. The meat or fish is then stir-fried in a clean wok and the vegetables are returned to the pan to heat through before serving.

Deep-Frying

You will find a wok ideal for deep-frying, though a regular saucepan will also do. Do not use a frying pan. It is too shallow and the oil will spatter over its rim. To deep-fry properly, there must be at least 1″ of oil in the pan. A Chinese strainer or a pair of cooking chopsticks simplifies the removal of cooked foods from the hot oil.

The correct temperature for the majority of deep-frying is from 325 to 350 degrees. A Chinese cook usually tests the temperature by placing a bamboo chopstick in the hot oil. If bubbles form around the chopstick, the oil is ready. Beware if the bubbles form very fast, however; this indicates that the oil is too hot. You may, of course, use a cooking thermometer, or test the temperature with a piece of bread or a thin slice of ginger. If the temperature is too high, the bread or ginger will burn within seconds.

When deep-frying meat or poultry, it is essential that the oil be the proper temperature. Needless to say, it is very unpleasant to bite into a crispy morsel and find that it is still raw in the center, which is what will happen if the oil is too hot. If foods are cooking too quickly on the outside or are burning, remove them to a 325-degree oven to cook through (about 10 to 15 minutes). You will also have problems if you add too much food to the oil at once. The temperature of the oil will drop and the food will take longer to cook. The result will be a plate of oil-soaked morsels.

Save the oil. It may be used several more times, especially if it has been kept to a temperature below 350 degrees. (High temperatures cause cooking oils to "break down" and become rancid very quickly.) As the oil cools, sediment will settle to the bottom of the pan. Simply pour the oil into a container, leaving the sediment behind. Store, covered, at room temperature.

Pan-Frying

The wok's concave shape makes it the perfect utensil for pan-frying. Greasy spatters are kept to a minimum and foods like noodles or rice can be tossed and stirred without fear of spilling them over the pan rim. Plus, a fried egg will come out perfectly round every time.

Pan-fry in a wok as you would in a skillet. Heat the pan and add 1 or 2 tablespoons oil. Add the food and cook over medium or medium-high heat. French toast, steaks and chops, chicken, and fish can all be cooked in this manner.

Steaming

Steaming preserves the natural juices and flavors of foods with little loss of vitamins or minerals. It is also a marvelous way to reheat leftovers without drying them out. In fact, a certain amount of condensed steam combines with the moisture in leftover foods to form a flavorful gravy.

Among the many popular dishes that are steamed are pork cake, prawns in black bean sauce, whole fish, and *deem sum* delicacies too numerous to mention. Steamed dishes are particularly easy to serve, as they usually can go directly from the steamer to the table with only the addition of a garnish.

No matter what steamer you use (see Cooking Utensils), the method remains essentially the same. Add hot water to the bottom section of the aluminum steamer (to 1″ below the rim) or to the wok (to within ½″ of the bottom of the steam plate or 1″ of the bamboo steamer). Bring the water to a boil over high heat. Arrange the food on a shallow dish or pie plate, and when the water boils, place the plate in the steamer, cover, and start timing. Be sure that the water continues to boil throughout the prescribed cooking time. When preparing foods that require long cooking, check the water level occasionally; if it has dropped, add boiling water to return it to the original level.

By the way, corn on the cob, steamed over high heat until tender, is absolutely delicious. Try it.

Stewing

Stewed dishes are especially flavorful when cooked in a wok. The shape of the pan serves to condense the steam and return it to the stew, thereby retaining the natural juices and full flavors of the ingredients. Cantonese-style beef stew and spareribs with black bean sauce or hoisin sauce are especially delicious when long-cooked in a wok.

Preparing stewed dishes in a wok is very simple. You need only remember to keep the heat at a medium or medium-low level and to cover the pan.

Reheating Leftovers in a Microwave Oven

The microwave oven permits the reheating of foods without drying them out. Cover the plate of leftovers with plastic wrap and place in the oven. Turn the setting to high and heat for 30 seconds to 2 minutes, depending on the quantity and density of the foods.

Using Marinades and Seasonings

Some recipes in this book call for marinades, others call for seasonings. Both add flavor to foods, but each is treated in a different way. Seasonings are usually added to the food shortly before cooking (although they *may* be added several hours ahead if you are completing preparation steps in advance of cooking). Marinades take a longer time, ideally at least 2 hours, to impart flavor. Marinate foods overnight in the refrigerator, if that is convenient for you.

Cornstarch is often a part of both mixtures, as it helps the flavors bond to the foods. For best results, sprinkle seasonings or marinade ingredients onto foods in the order given, then mix well. This is especially important if cornstarch is one of the ingredients.

Thickeners

The standard thickener in Chinese cooking is 1 part cornstarch (or tapioca starch) to 2 parts water. This ratio will vary depending on how much liquid is being thickened and how thin it is to start.

To thicken the sauce in a stir-fry dish, shove the food to one side of the wok. Stir the thickener well and then pour *some* of it slowly into the liquid remaining at the center of the wok. Cook for about 30 seconds without stirring (stirring reduces the temperature of the mixture). Now check to see if the liquid is the desired consistency. If it is still too thin, add more of the thickener and cook a bit longer. If it is too thick, add a little hot water. When the consistency is just right, stir the food into the liquid and serve.

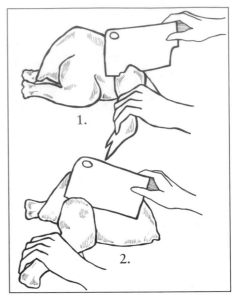

How to Bone Chicken

CUTTING TECHNIQUES

How to Bone a Chicken

Students in my cooking classes often ask me to show them how to bone a chicken, so I have included the instructions here. Boned chicken is used in many of my recipes, and for greater economy, I recommend buying a whole chicken instead of chicken parts or chicken that has been boned by the butcher. A comparison of price per pound reveals that you are paying dearly for these conveniences.

Here is how I arrive at large, good-sized pieces of boned chicken meat. With a little practice, you will be able to perform these same steps very quickly.

1. Place the chicken on the chopping board breast down with its head pointing right. Grasp the wing nearest you firmly, then cut through the joint where it joins the body. (To find the joint, probe gently with the edge of the cleaver blade.) Turn chicken 180 degrees and repeat with the other wing.
2. Find the joint where the leg joins the body, again by probing gently with cleaver blade. Remove both legs in the same manner in which you removed the wings.

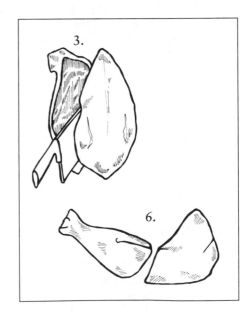

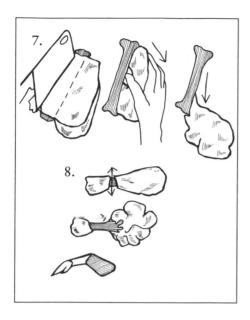

3. Remove the tail and any fat. Grasp the carcass near the tail, with its back against your palm. Stand the bird firmly on its head. Cleave the carcass into 2 parts, the back and the breast. (You will find that the bones along this plane are small and easily cut through with the cleaver.) Since the back has little meat, set it aside for making soup stock.

4. Remove the skin from the chicken breast by grasping it with your hand and pulling it away from the flesh. Cut along the right side of the breastbone as close to the bone as possible. Turn chicken breast 180 degrees and do the same on the other side.

5. Now pull the meat away from the carcass with your fingers. You can hold the cleaver blade tightly against the carcass to keep the chicken in place as you pull.

6. Separate the thighs from the drumsticks by cutting at the joint. Remove the skin from the thighs by pulling it free with your hand.

7. Place a thigh on the cutting board, skin side down. Make 2 cuts, one along each side of the bone. Grasp the 2 resulting flaps of meat in your hand and pull them to one side. While holding onto the meat, poke the index finger of your other hand between the flesh and the bone about midway up the bone and work your finger up and down the bone to free the meat. Use the cleaver to cut the meat free at the end where it attaches to the bone. Repeat with the other thigh.

8. Remove skin from drumsticks by pulling it free with your hand. Make a circular cut, through the meat to the bone, at the narrow end of the drumstick.

9. Grasp the small end of the drumstick with one hand. With the other hand, free the meat by working your fingers along the bone. (Warning: Be careful not to poke yourself on the needlelike bone attached at the large end of the drumstick.) Cut meat free where it is attached to the bone. Repeat with other drumstick.

10. The only meaty part of the wing is the large portion nearest the body of the chicken. It resembles a drumstick in miniature, hence it is commonly called a "drumette." Remove the wing tip by cutting through the joint and set it aside for stock. Leaving the skin on, bone the drumette as you did the drumstick. Because of its smaller size, the meat may be freed from the bone by simply working it loose with your fingers. Push the meat to the top of the bone, but leave it attached. The bone is then a convenient handle when served.

How to Slice Chicken

This is how chicken is cut for the majority of my recipes. When other dimensions are required, they are specified in the recipe methods.

1. Slice a boned and skinned chicken breast crosswise into strips ½″ wide. The resulting pieces will be about 1½″ by ½″.

2. Cut the thigh meat lengthwise into strips ½″ wide. These pieces will also be about 1½″ by ½″.

3. The meat from the drumsticks will not be regular in shape and will have tears. Cut lengthwise to form pieces as close as possible in size to those for breast and thigh sections.

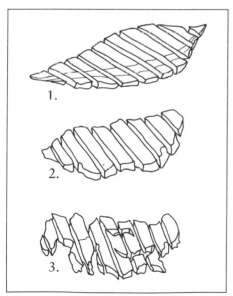

How to Slice Chicken

How to Shell and Devein Prawns

1. Starting at the head end, pull the shell loose from the prawn. Pull off the tail; this must be done somewhat gently so that the delicate tail portions are not snapped off with the shell.
2. Cut a shallow impression along the back (outside curve) of the prawn with scissors or a cleaver. Wash the prawn under cold running water, easing the dark vein out with your fingertips. (This vein often contains grit and must be removed. The small vein on the inside curve need not be removed.) Drain and pat dry before cooking.

How to Slice Flank Steak

Flank steak is the beef cut most commonly used in stir-frying because it is tender, flavorful, and relatively free of fat. (Skirt steak may also be used.) When combined with vegetables and served in the Chinese manner, one average-sized flank steak, weighing about 1½ lb., will suffice for 4 to 6 persons, making it a particularly economical choice as well. To facilitate cutting, partially freeze the flank steak (about 2 hours) to firm the meat.

1. Cut the flank steak lengthwise (with grain of meat) into 3 equal strips each approximately 1½" wide.
2. Cut each strip across the grain into slices less than ¼" thick.

How to Clean and Cut Squid

1. Cut off the head from the body of the squid just below the eyes. Cut off and discard the portion containing the eyes. Reserve the tentacles (they are the best part!) in one piece. With a thin-bladed knife or your finger, "pop out" the small round of cartilage embedded in the base of the tentacles.
2. Slit the body lengthwise. Remove the bladelike cartilage and the entrails and discard. Peel off mottled skin, using your fingers or a small knife. Wash, drain, and pat squid dry with paper towels.
3. Place squid body on cutting board, outside down. Score (do not cut all the way through) entire body every ¼" on the diagonal. Turn squid and score at right angles to the first cuts every ¼". This will make the squid body curl during cooking.
4. Cut squid crosswise into pieces 1½" wide.

How to Prepare Vegetables

When vegetables are called for in recipes, a brief explanation of how to prepare them is provided. Here I am supplying more specific instructions for vegetables that are repeatedly referred to, especially if they are cut in a manner different from that usually prescribed in Chinese cooking. For instance, many Chinese cooks simply cut celery stalks crosswise on the diagonal, while I prefer to cut them in julienne and have designed my recipes to accommodate this change.

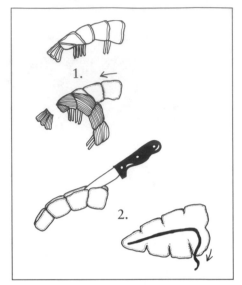

Prawns

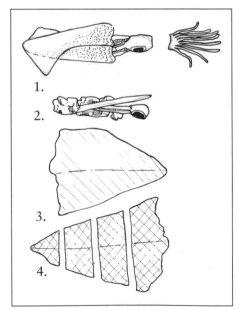

Squid

The principal aim when preparing vegetables is to cut them in such a way that a maximum amount of surface is exposed to the heat, allowing the pieces to cook very quickly. This way the vegetables remain crisp and flavorful, while at the same time you conserve fuel. Sometimes a recipe calls for all the ingredients to be cut into the same size and shape. There are two reasons for this: a similarity in size means that all the ingredients will cook in the same amount of time and, secondly, the finished dish will be more pleasing to the eye.

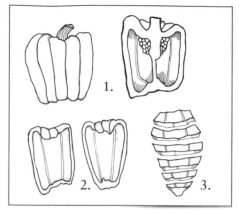

Bell Pepper

Asparagus
1. Break off and discard tough base end of stalk.
2. Starting at tip end of spear, cut spear at ½″ intervals on the diagonal. The resulting slices should have no part thicker than ½″ and an overall length of 1½″.

Bell Pepper
1. Cut bell pepper in half. Remove and discard stem and seeds.
2. Place each half on cutting board, cut side up. Cut lengthwise into strips 1¼″ wide.
3. Cut each strip crosswise into ¼″ pieces. Each piece will be 1¼″ by ¼″.

Broccoli
1. Remove tough covering on stalks by inserting a knife blade under the skin. Put your thumb on the flat of the blade and pull the skin away. (It is usually necessary to peel only the bottom 3½″ of the stalk. The top part is tender enough without peeling.)
2. Cut stalk in half crosswise.
3. Cut bottom part of stalk in half lengthwise. Cut each piece at ⅓″ intervals on the diagonal. Each slice should be approximately ⅓″ thick and 1½″ long.
4. Break flowerets off top part of stalk. Leave whole if small; cut in half if large.
5. Cut top part of stalk in the manner described in step 3.

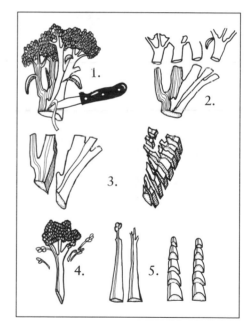

Broccoli

Bok Choy
1. Break off branches surrounding center stalk. Remove and discard root end of stalk and any flowers.
2. Cut branches on the diagonal into pieces 1″ wide. Cut leaves into 2″ lengths.
3. Peel tough exterior from center stalk by inserting a small knife blade under the skin. Hold your thumb against the flat of the blade and pull the skin away.
4. Cut center stalk on the diagonal into slices ⅓″ thick and 1½″ long.

Celery
1. Lightly pare the outside of the celery stalk with a vegetable peeler to remove the stringy fibers. This makes every stalk taste young and tender.
2. Holding the knife at a 30-degree angle to the stalk, cut the stalk into pieces 1½″ long.
3. Cut each piece lengthwise into thin strips, julienne style.

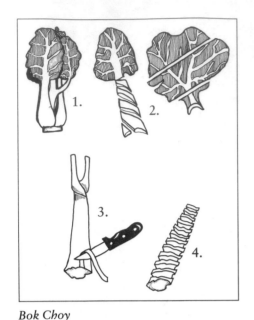

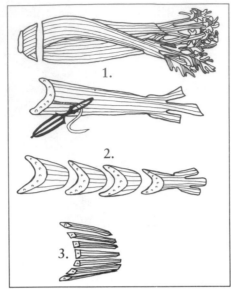

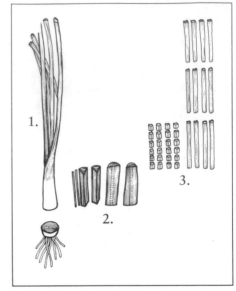

Bok Choy   Celery   Green Onion

Green Onion

Green onions are incorporated into many Chinese dishes. The entire onion is used. Both the green and white sections impart flavor; the colorful tops also make the dish more attractive. The onions are slivered or diced, depending upon the dish.

1. Trim off the root end. Cut whole onion into 1½″ lengths.
2. Cut each piece in half lengthwise, then into quarters to make slivers.
3. If the recipe calls for diced onions, cut the slivers crosswise into ⅛″ pieces.

Snow Pea

1. Trim off tips of snow peas.
2. Cut peas in half on the diagonal.

Yellow Onion

1. Trim off stem and base ends of onion. Cut in half lengthwise. Peel halves.
2. Place halves cut side down. Cut each half lengthwise into slices or wedges ¼″ thick.
3. If recipe calls for diced yellow onion, cut each slice crosswise into ¼″ cubes.

Zucchini

1. Trim off stem and blossom ends of zucchini. Cut in half lengthwise.
2. Cut on the diagonal into slices ¼″ thick.

Ingredients Used in Chinese Cooking

Baby Corn Ears
See corn ears, baby.

冬筍 **Bamboo Shoots**
For best appearance and flavor, buy canned whole "winter bamboo shoots" packed in water. Canned bamboo shoots are also available sliced. Refrigerate unused shoots in water to cover in a covered container for up to 2 weeks; change the water every 3 days.

Barbecued Pork
See pork, barbecued.

腐乳 **Bean Cake, Fermented**
Because of the natural fermentation process, these strong-flavored bean cake cubes will keep, refrigerated, for up to 2 years. They come packed in 16-oz. jars and are used in stir-fried vegetable dishes, with meats, clams, and boiled chicken, and, with a little sugar added, as an accompaniment to plain steamed rice.

豆腐 **Bean Cake, Fresh**
My recipes call for firm bean cake. Don't buy the smooth style that comes in a single thick slab. It is too soft for stir-frying. Both types are sold in plastic containers found in the cold case in the supermarket; each package has an expiration date stamped on the top to guarantee freshness (they should be used immediately, however). Drain bean cake, rinse with cold water, and drain again before using. To store, drain, cover with water, and refrigerate for no more than 2 days. Bean cake is an excellent source of protein. Bland in taste, it readily absorbs the flavors of the foods with which it is cooked.

紅腐乳 **Bean Curd, Preserved Red**
This product is a mixture of red rice and soybeans, and should not be confused with fermented or fresh bean cakes. It is used in small quantities for flavoring beef and duck stews and in a vegetarian dish traditionally served at Chinese New Year celebrations. It comes packed in brine in 8-oz. cans. To store, remove to a covered jar and refrigerate. It will keep indefinitely.

磨豉醬 豆 **Bean Sauce**
Available in cans or jars, bean sauce comes in several different styles. Cantonese bean sauce is mild in flavor, and is labeled "bean sauce" or sometimes "ground bean sauce." With sugar added, it becomes "sweet bean paste," which is often used as a condiment with Peking duck or mo shu dishes. Szechuan bean sauce has chili peppers added, and is usually labeled "hot bean sauce." If any of these sauces are purchased in a can, remove to a jar. Bean sauce will keep in the refrigerator in a covered container for 2 years.

芽菜 **Bean Sprouts**
This tasty, inexpensive vegetable adds flavor and texture to many dishes. The sprouts usually found in grocery stores are from the small green mung bean and require almost no cooking. They should be firm and shiny, never limp or in the least bit brown. They will keep in a plastic bag in the refrigerator for about 2 days. The larger soybean sprouts are sometimes available. They require longer cooking and are usually used in braised rather than stir-fried dishes.

粉絲 **Bean Threads**
Made from mung-bean starch, these noodles are wiry and white before cooking and are often mistaken for rice sticks, which they resemble. When cooked, usually in soups or stir-fry dishes, they become soft and translucent. They are also called "long rice" and "cellophane noodles." Store at room temperature in a closed container for up to 2 years.

豆豉 **Black Beans, Salted**
Packed in plastic bags or in boxes, usually with salt crystals easily visible, salted black beans are somewhat soft in texture. They are easily confused with the hard dried black beans, used in soups, which come in similar packages. Salted black beans are used to make the black bean sauce that is frequently served with spareribs, prawns, lobster, and chicken. Stored in a covered jar in the refrigerator, they will keep for 2 years.

Black Fungus, Dried
See fungus, dried black.

Black Mushrooms, Chinese Dried
See mushrooms, Chinese dried black.

白菜 **Bok Choy**
This popular Chinese vegetable has long, smooth greenish stalks topped by dark green leaves. It is available year-round, is inexpensive, and since the entire bok choy, including the heart, is edible, is a particularly good buy. There is also a "baby bok choy" now in markets, which is about 6″ long and especially delightful. This vegetable often appears on Chinese menus as "Chinese greens." Will keep in the refrigerator in a plastic bag for up to 2 weeks.

黄糖 **Brown Sugar Bars**
Brown sugar pressed into a hard bar. Although it looks like regular brown sugar, it has a different flavor. Used in Chinese doughnuts, braised pigs' feet, and other dishes.

Cabbage, Napa
See Napa cabbage.

Candied Winter Melon
See winter melon.

腰果 **Cashew Nuts, Raw**
Purchase cashews in plastic bags or in bulk in Asian grocery stores or in health-food stores. Store in a covered container at room temperature for up to 6 months, or in the refrigerator for up to a year. Cashews may be used interchangeably with almonds in many recipes. If raw cashews are unavailable, use unsalted roasted cashews; skip the step in recipes that calls for roasting the nuts.

鷄湯 **Chicken Stock**
Canned chicken stock or chicken stock base may be used. The best chicken stock, however, is the kind you make yourself. Simmer a chicken carcass and a slice of fresh ginger root in 2 qt. water for 30 minutes. Add salt and thin soy sauce to taste. Strain. Store in the refrigerator for up to 4 days, or for up to 2 months in the freezer.

蒜蓉辣醬 **Chili Paste with Garlic**
A bottle paste made from chili peppers, garlic, and salt, this pungent mixture is used in many Szechuan dishes. Refrigerated, it will keep for 2 to 3 years.

Chili Pepper, Dried Red
See pepper, dried red chili.

甜辣醬 **Chili Sauce, Sweet**
A piquant, spicy sauce a bit like catsup, this bottled import from Singapore is quite new in the markets. Use it as a dipping sauce or condiment. Store at room temperature for up to 2 years.

Chinese Dried Black Mushrooms
See mushrooms, Chinese dried black.

Chinese Fresh Noodles
See noodles, Chinese fresh.

臘腸 **Chinese Sausage**
Available loose or packed in cellophane, these sausages are reddish in color and resemble long link sausage. They come in three "flavors," beef, pork, and duck liver. I suggest you buy pork because I think you are more apt to like it. Many people, including some Chinese, don't like the strong flavors of the others. These sausages are stir-fried or steamed with rice, chopped and used in steamed meat cakes, or added to poultry stuffings. Refrigerated, they will keep for up to 3 months. They may also be frozen for up to 6 months.

玉米筍 **Corn Ears, Baby**
Used in stir-fry dishes, stews, and soups, these tiny ears of corn (some are only about 2″ long) are cooked by a canning process. Rinse unused corn in cold water and store in water to cover in a covered container in the refrigerator for up to 10 days; change the water every 3 days.

豆粉 **Cornstarch**
This powdered corn product is used as a thickener in gravies, in deep-fry batters, and in marinades to give meats a smooth texture. In most recipes, tapioca starch may be substituted. Cornstarch will keep in a dry place at room temperature for 2 years.

咖喱 **Curry Powder**
"Madras" curry powder provides the flavor I seek for my curry recipes. Any imported curry powder may be substituted. Keep curry powder at room temperature indefinitely; the flavor will diminish over a long period, however.

紅棗 **Dates, Red**
These dried Chinese dates, also called "jujube dates," are used in soups and steamed dishes to impart a sweet flavor. To use, soak for 10 minutes in warm water to cover. Remove pits and check insides for possible spoilage. Use whole or cut lengthwise into strips. Store at room temperature for up to 1 year.

Deep-Fried Noodles
See noodles, deep-fried.

Dried Black Fungus
See fungus, dried black.

Dried Chinese Black Mushrooms
See mushrooms, Chinese dried black.

Dried Lily Flowers
See lily flowers, dried.

Dried Red Chili Pepper
See pepper, dried red chili.

Dried Seaweed
See seaweed, dried.

茄子 **Eggplant, Oriental**
This beautiful, purple-skinned vegetable is about 6″ long and 1½″ thick. It is picked younger than globe eggplant and is therefore more tender. Globe eggplant may be substituted if the slender variety is not available. Eggplant will keep about 10 days in the refrigerator.

春捲皮 **Egg Roll Skins**
Very thin sheets of dough about 6″ square. They come in 1-lb. packages and are usually found in the supermarket cold case. Look for Ho Tai, Chinese Inn, Menlo, or Doll Brand; they are all very thin wrappers and thus make a crisper egg roll. Because they are so thin, they are a little harder to separate, but the added quality is worth the few extra moments. Store unused skins in a plastic bag in the refrigerator for 1 week, or freeze for up to 2 months. Defrost for at least 5 hours before using.

Fermented Bean Cake
See bean cake, fermented.

五香粉 **Five-Spice Powder**
A ready-mixed spice blend of fennel seed, Szechuan or "anise" peppercorns, star anise, cinnamon, and cloves. It may be purchased in small amounts in plastic bags. Very pungent, five-spice powder is used sparingly when roasting or stewing meat or poultry. It is the "flavor" of "flavored salt," which is used in Cantonese chicken salad and as a condiment with deep-fried poultry. Keeps indefinitely in a tightly covered jar at room temperature.

Fresh Bean Cake
See bean cake, fresh.

Fresh Chinese Noodles
See noodles, fresh Chinese.

Fresh Ginger Root
See ginger root, fresh.

木耳 **Fungus, Dried Black**
This relative of the mushroom, which has almost no taste of its own, is used for its delightfully crunchy texture. It goes by several other names, including tree fungus and wood ears. When soaked in warm water, it increases to 4 times its original size. Black fungus is used in many stir-fry and mo shu dishes and in hot-and-sour soup. Sold by weight in plastic bags, it will keep a few years in a dry place.

蒜子 **Garlic**
Whenever possible, buy loose garlic rather than buds or cloves packed in plastic. The unbagged buds and cloves are often bigger and are often better quality. To peel, place a clove on a chopping surface and crush it slightly with a slap of the side of the cleaver. The loosened skin will slide away between your fingers. Whole garlic keeps at room temperature for months if left exposed to the air. Do not wrap!

薑 **Ginger Root, Fresh**
Now available in most supermarkets, fresh ginger adds a distinctive flavor and aroma to many dishes. (You do not need to purchase the whole root; just snap off the portion you need.) Store unwrapped in a cool, dry place for up to 2 months. Do not wash more than you need at the moment. Peel before using.

Glutinous Rice
See rice, sweet.

糯米粉 **Glutinous Rice Flour**
This flour, or powder, is made from glutinous rice and is used for desserts and some savory dishes. Check that the label specifies "glutinous" or "sweet" rice when purchasing, to avoid error. Will keep for 1 year at room temperature.

Ground Pork
See pork, ground.

海 鮮 醬 **Hoisin Sauce**
A popular sweet, reddish sauce commonly used as a condiment with Peking duck and mo shu pork, it comes in 16-oz. jars or cans. If purchased in a can, transfer to a covered glass container after opening. It will keep for up to 2 years in the refrigerator.

豆 瓣 醬 **Hot Bean Sauce**
See bean sauce.

辣 油 **Hot Oil**
Available bottled, this oil, used as a condiment, is found on the tables of most Chinese restaurants. Also known as chili oil, it is quite spicy and should be used with caution. The homemade version, which uses safflower oil, is preferable, since there is no "greasy" aftertaste. A recipe for hot oil appears in the Appetizers chapter.

蕃 葛 **Jicama**
An excellent substitute for water chestnuts, jicama has a sweet taste and crisp texture. Eaten raw like an apple, it makes a good, low-calorie snack. Look for it in the vegetable section of most supermarkets. Jicama is shaped like a beet and has coarse brown skin, similar in appearance to potato skin; the flesh looks like that of raw potato. Size varies from about ¼ lb. to 4 times that weight. Cut off only the amount you plan to use, then wash and peel it. Store unused portion in the crisper of your refrigerator in a plastic bag with the top open. It will keep for about 2 weeks.

耶 菜 頭 **Kohlrabi**
A vegetable shaped like a turnip, with a thick green skin. It may be eaten raw and is delicious when stir-fried. Keeps for 1 week in the refrigerator.

金 針 **Lily Flowers, Dried**
Also known as "golden needle" because of the shape and color, each lily flower is about 3″ long. Soak in warm water to cover for 10 minutes, then cut off and discard ½″ from the pointed end of each needle (this part is very tough). Sold in plastic bags at Chinese groceries. Lily flowers will keep 1 year at room temperature.

青 豆 角 **Long Beans**
These look like ordinary string beans, except that they are about 2 feet long. They come tied in bundles (you need not buy the whole bundle) and are now starting to be seen in supermarkets. Their season is from May to September. Except for the tip ends, the entire bean is used, most often in a stir-fry. Store in the refrigerator for up to 10 days.

蓮 藕 **Lotus Root**
This tuberous stem of the lotus plant, about 8″ long and 2″ in diameter, looks like a dahlia tuber. Cut crosswise, the lotus becomes lovely lacey slices. Cut lengthwise, the root forms delicate threads. It is used in soups and adds a crisp texture to stir-fry dishes. Dried and sweetened, it is eaten as a confection and used to sweeten tea on special occasions. It will keep for 2 weeks in the refrigerator.

冬 菇 **Mushrooms, Chinese Dried Black**
These mushrooms have a very distinctive flavor and add considerably to many dishes. Although somewhat expensive by the pound, they are very light, and the smaller, less expensive ones may be used for any recipe calling for chopped or sliced mushrooms. Before using, soak in warm water to cover for 30 minutes, or boil in water to cover for 10 minutes. Rinse and squeeze dry, then remove and discard the stems. Stored in a tightly covered container in the refrigerator, dried mushrooms will keep for 2 years.

草 菇 **Mushrooms, Straw**
These conical, subtly flavored mushrooms are similar in size to button mushrooms. They come, either peeled or unpeeled, in 16-oz. cans. Store unused mushrooms in water to cover in a covered container in the refrigerator, changing the water every 3 days. They will keep about 10 days.

芥 菜 **Mustard Greens, Chinese**
Similar in size to an American head cabbage, these greens, also called mustard cabbage, are deep colored and have fanlike leaves. A smallish variety is used principally in soups; heads with thicker stalks are good for pickling (see recipe for Pickled Mustard Greens in Vegetables chapter).

芥 辣 **Mustard Powder**
This fine yellow powder is used for making the hot-mustard condiment served with many dishes. Look for it in Chinese markets. Coleman brand English-style dry mustard may also be used. Mix equal amounts of mustard powder and cold water; if a smoother consistency is desired, add 1 or 2 drops of oil.

紹 菜 **Napa Cabbage**
This inexpensive, sweet-tasting, cylindrically shaped vegetable is also known as Chinese celery cabbage or Chinese lettuce. Its crisp, tightly packed leaves are very nutritious. They are primarily used in stir-fry dishes and in soups. The entire head, except for the tough stalk portion, is used. Napa cabbage will keep in the refrigerator for up to 2 weeks.

長壽麵 Noodles, Deep-Fried

These noodles, called *yee mein* ("long-life noodles"), are traditionally served at birthday celebrations to wish the honoree a long life. They are deep-fried, pressed into 8-oz. disks about 8" in diameter and 2" thick, and then packaged in a plastic bag. (Do not confuse these noodles with noodles used for chow mein, which are also deep-fried but look like shoestring potatoes.) *Yee mein* must be parboiled before serving. They will keep about 2 weeks at room temperature.

麵 Noodles, Fresh Chinese

Available in 1-lb. packages at most Asian markets and many supermarkets, fresh Chinese wheat noodles come in many different widths and are usually labeled simply "Chinese noodles." The fine, almost hairlike noodles and those about ¼" wide are used in soup. Noodles about ⅛" wide are used for pan-frying. Fresh noodles will keep refrigerated for about 10 days, or they may be frozen for up to 2 months. Defrost frozen noodles for several hours at room temperature before cooking.

Nuts, Raw Cashew

See cashew nuts, raw.

油 Oil

Use any free-flowing, unsaturated oil, such as safflower, corn, peanut, or vegetable oil, for all your Chinese cooking needs.

Oil, Sesame

See sesame oil.

Oriental Eggplant

See eggplant, Oriental.

蠔油 Oyster Sauce

This sauce, made from oysters, salt, starch, and caramel coloring, has a distinctive, but not fishy, flavor. It is an important ingredient in cooking and is also used as a condiment (it makes a great steak sauce). The more expensive brands are definitely superior in flavor and worth the extra cost. Recommended brands are Hop Sing Lum and Lee Kum Kee (on the latter, look for the "Old Brand" label showing a woman and child in a boat, in preference to the new red-and-white label). Once opened, oyster sauce can be stored in the refrigerator for up to 2 years.

去衣花生 Peanuts, Raw

May be purchased in Chinese groceries or in health-food stores. Buy the shelled and skinned variety. They will keep for about 6 months in a covered container at room temperature, or for up to 1 year in the refrigerator. If unavailable, use unsalted roasted peanuts; skip the step in the recipes that calls for toasting the peanuts.

辣椒 **Pepper, Dried Red Chili**
These can be found whole or finely chopped in plastic bags at the supermarket or
Chinese grocery. They will keep in a covered container at room temperature for up
to 1 year; after that point the flavor begins to diminish.

叉燒 **Pork, Barbecued**
Sold by the piece at Chinese take-out food stores or make your own (see Meat
chapter). Barbecued pork will keep in the refrigerator for 1 week, or may be frozen
for 3 months.

碎豬肉 **Pork, Ground**
Grind your own, using pork shoulder, butt, or loin (don't use pork chops, as they
are too dry), in your food processor or ask the butcher to grind it for you. Be sure
to trim off excess fat before grinding. Ground pork will keep about 2 days in the
refrigerator, or for up to 3 months in the freezer.

鍋貼皮 **Pot Sticker Skins**
Pot sticker skins are 3″ in diameter and come about 35 skins to a 1-lb. package.
Do not confuse with *sui mai* skins or *suey gow* skins, which are thinner. Wrapped
in a plastic bag, the skins will keep for 1 week in the refrigerator, or for up to
2 months in the freezer. Defrost frozen skins at room temperature for at least 5
hours before using.

Preserved Red Bean Curd
See bean curd, preserved red.

津冬菜 **Preserved Vegetables, Tientsin**
Cabbage preserved with garlic and salt, packed in a clay pot. The cabbage adds
flavor to pot stickers, steamed fish, pork cake, and other dishes. Store in the refrigerator, with aluminum foil over the opening, for up to 2 years.

Raw Cashew Nuts
See cashew nuts, raw.

Raw Peanuts
See peanuts, raw.

Red Chili Pepper, Dried
See pepper, dried red chili.

Red Dates
See dates, red.

米 **Rice, Long-Grain**
This is the rice preferred for everyday eating by the Chinese. It is available in Chinese markets in sacks weighing from 10 to 50 lb. each. One favorite brand is "AA," from Texas. Raw rice should be rinsed well in at least 4 changes of water before cooking to remove starch. Put it in a pan with plenty of water and swish it around with your hand. Drain and repeat 3 times, or until water remains clear. (If using "converted," or precooked, rice, follow the instructions on the package.) Store in a covered container at room temperature for up to 1 year.

Rice, Short-Grain
日本米 This rice, which is slightly sticky when cooked, is used for making the patties for sizzling rice soup. It is the type preferred for everyday eating by the Japanese. Calrose brand is from California; Japanese brands include Botan and Kokuko Rose. Wash and store as for long-grain rice.

糯米 **Rice, Sweet**
Sweet rice, also called "glutinous rice," is used for sweet-rice rolls, eight precious pudding, and Chinese tamales (*joong*). It has a shiny appearance when cooked. Wash and store as for long-grain rice.

排米粉 **Rice Sticks**
Rice sticks are dried noodles made from rice flour, blander in flavor than wheat noodles. There are two basic types. The threadlike noodles that resemble (and are often confused with) bean threads are often deep-fried for use in such popular dishes as Cantonese-style chicken salad and Mongolian beef. They may be labeled *py mei fun* or simply rice sticks. A variety about ¼" wide, usually labeled dried rice sticks, is used in soups and stir-fried dishes (*chow fun*). Store at room temperature in a plastic bag for up to 2 years.

醋 **Rice Vinegar**
Marukan rice vinegar, a Japanese brand, comes in 12-oz. and 25-oz. bottles and will keep for 2 years at room temperature. I use this vinegar because it is available in most supermarkets and I like the flavor. Buy the green-labeled, unseasoned variety, which contains no MSG. The variety with the orange label is seasoned and is too strong for Chinese dishes. There are also Chinese rice vinegars. Red rice vinegar is used as a condiment with steamed crab. Black rice vinegar has the viscosity of molasses. It is used in a classic Chinese pigs' feet recipe.

燒鹽 **Roasting Salt**
This is a necessary ingredient for Chinese barbecued pork, both for flavor and red color. It is very inexpensive and may be purchased in Chinese markets. Keeps indefinitely at room temperature in a closed container.

Sausage, Chinese
See Chinese sausage.

Salted Black Beans
See black beans, salted.

紫菜 **Seaweed, Dried**
Used mainly in soup. One variety available in broad, flat sheets, resembles crinkled brown paper. It comes in 2-oz. cellophane packages sometimes labeled dried laver and is relatively inexpensive. Hair seaweed, which looks like upholsterer's horsehair, is another form and is quite expensive. Its Chinese name is *fat choy*, and it is in great demand at Chinese New Year's when the traditional greeting is *"Gung hay fat choy."* Chinese enjoy the play on words. Dried seaweed keeps for up to 2 years in a dry place at room temperature.

芝麻油 **Sesame Oil**
This amber flavoring oil made from toasted sesame seeds lends zest to cold plates, stir-fry and noodle dishes, and soups. It is very fragrant, so should be used sparingly. Do not substitute the paler variety sold in supermarkets and health-food stores. Once opened, store it in the refrigerator, or it will become rancid.

芝麻 **Sesame Seeds**
White sesame seeds are frequently used in Chinese cooking for added flavor and texture. Buy them in cellophane bags at a Chinese grocery and toast them yourself for fresher flavor. Black sesame seeds are also available, and are used to make a sweet pudding and to decorate buns. Both types will keep for several months in an airtight container at room temperature.

Short-Grain Rice
See rice, short-grain.

蘭豆 **Snow Peas**
Used in many dishes for its bright green color, crispy texture, and delightful flavor, the snow pea must be everyone's favorite Chinese vegetable. Picked before the peas mature, the entire pod is eaten (the flatter the pod, the younger and more tender the pea). Snow peas are available all year long, but are prohibitively expensive during the winter months. They will keep in the refrigerator in a plastic bag for about 10 days.

生抽 **Soy Sauce**
老抽 Made from soybeans, salt, sugar, flour, and water, this savory brown sauce is used to add flavor to many Chinese dishes. Soy sauce will keep for several months at room temperature, or for up to 2 years in the refrigerator. There are two basic kinds of soy sauce. Thin soy sauce, sometimes called light soy sauce, is used for seasoning and as a table condiment. It is reddish in color and has a "watery" consistency. Dark soy sauce, also called black soy sauce, is sweeter and has a syrupy consistency. It is used for coloring gravies and for flavoring fried rice. It is sometimes difficult to tell from the label which kind is in the container, unless you read Chinese. For example, one common brand, Pearl River Bridge, labels its thin soy sauce Superior Soy, while the dark soy carries the label Soy Superior. If in doubt, ask the clerk.

八角 **Star Anise**
A star-shaped pod with a licorice flavor, star anise is one of the elements of five-spice powder and is used to flavor stews. Whole pods have 5 or 6 points. Sold in small cellophane bags, the pods are often broken, so you may need to estimate the equivalent of a whole pod. Star anise will keep indefinitely in a covered container at room temperature.

Straw Mushrooms
See mushrooms, straw.

Sweet Rice
See rice, sweet.

Sweet Chili Sauce
See chili sauce, sweet.

菱粉 **Tapioca Starch**
A dry starch that can be substituted for cornstarch for thickening liquids. It makes a slightly thicker sauce than cornstarch. It is widely used in the Orient, where cornstarch is not as readily available. Store for up to 2 years at room temperature.

茶葉 **Tea**
Tea is known to have been used medicinally and for restorative purposes over 2,000 years ago. Ever present in the Chinese household, it is brewed fresh each morning and kept hot in a vacuum bottle or in a pot cradled in a wicker basket. It is drunk throughout the day and is always offered to guests as a sign of hospitality.

There are many different kinds of tea, each with its own distinctive flavor and aroma. They are classified as either strong or mild, and the expert tea drinker will select his tea to suit the state of his health, choosing a mild tea on a day when he or she feels poorly and a stronger one when feeling vigorous. A milder type, such as oolong or jasmine, is recommended for everyday use, but when having tea lunch in a restaurant, try a more exotic brew. The waiter will ask, *"Yum meh chah?"* ("What kind of tea?") Ask for *po nay,* lychee, *ti kuan yin,* or *look on.*

To make good tea, there are four things you need to remember: (1) the water must be boiling, (2) the proper measure is 1 tsp. dry tea for each qt. water, (3) the tea leaves go in the pot first, then the boiling water, and (4) the tea must steep for at least 5 minutes before serving.

Chinese teas are taken "as is"; sugar, lemon, or cream is never added. Dry tea keeps indefinitely in a cool place and improves with age.

Tientsin Preserved Vegetables
See preserved vegetables, Tientsin.

Vinegar, Rice
See rice vinegar.

馬蹄粉 **Water Chestnut Powder**

Sometimes called water chestnut starch, this is indeed made from water chestnuts. It is grainier than cornstarch and has a slightly "muddy" look when mixed with water. Water chestnut powder is used mostly in batters for deep-frying. Packaged in 8-oz. boxes, it will keep indefinitely in a dry place at room temperature.

馬蹄 **Water Chestnuts**

Fresh water chestnuts are imported from Hong Kong. They have the texture of a crisp apple and are delicious raw or cooked. They add flavor and a crunchy texture to stir-fry dishes, won ton fillings, and meat cakes. Wash, then remove and discard top and bottom with a sharp knife. Peel with a vegetable peeler, rinse, and place in cold water to prevent discoloration. They will keep (immersed in water) in the refrigerator for 2 days. Unpeeled, they will keep in the refrigerator for about 2 weeks.

When fresh water chestnuts are not available, jicama makes an excellent substitute. Canned water chestnuts are the next best alternative. Already peeled, they lose flavor and crispness during processing, but still add texture to stir-fry dishes. You may improve the flavor by sprinkling them with a little sugar while stir-frying in a small amount of oil. Store unused canned water chestnuts in water to cover in the refrigerator for up to 2 weeks, changing the water every 3 days.

紹興酒 **Wine**

Small amounts of wine are used in cooking poultry and seafoods for flavor and, in the case of fish and shellfish, to cut the "fishy" taste as well. Rice wine (Shao Shing is good), a dry white wine like sauterne, or a dry sherry may be used.

冬瓜 **Winter Melon**

Resembling a frosty watermelon, a winter melon is large, light green in color, and covered with a fine white powder. The meat is white and very delicate. Winter melons are in the market year-round, and a whole one will keep for several months in a cool place. This melon may also be purchased by the piece, which will keep about 1 week in the refrigerator. Fresh winter melon is used in soup or stir-fried as a vegetable; dried and sugared, it is a confection and is used for sweetening tea on special occasions.

雲吞皮 **Won Ton Skins**

Available in 1-lb. packages containing about 80 3½"-square skins. Store in a plastic bag in the refrigerator for up to 1 week, or freeze for up to 3 months. Defrost frozen skins at least 5 hours at room temperature before using.

How to Plan a Chinese Menu

Because of the tremendous variety of Chinese dishes, menu selection is often very confusing to the novice Chinese cook. The following guidelines should simplify planning a meal at home or ordering dinner at a restaurant.

A convenient rule of thumb is to serve one dish per person plus rice. When I state that a recipe "serves 4," I am assuming this is the formula you will follow. You can adjust a menu to suit your family's appetite by adding a soup or substituting one for a more filling dish.

Customarily, dishes are selected from each of several categories, such as meat, fish, vegetables, and so on, but this depends on your personal taste. If you are especially fond of seafood, choose from that category alone. Deep-fried shrimp and steamed whole fish are, after all, completely different. The dishes should complement each other, but the most important consideration is that you like them.

I strongly advise that you do not attempt more than two stir-fried dishes at one meal. Since these must be cooked at the last minute and served immediately, two is the limit one cook can handle easily. Using different cooking methods will also add diversity to your meal.

Lastly, do not omit rice or a rice substitute. This is the element that prevents the "Chinese food syndrome" of being hungry half an hour after the meal is finished. You may serve simple steamed rice, a more elaborate fried rice, or noodles, steamed buns, or other starchy food.

The Chinese do not usually eat dessert, but if the meal seems incomplete without one, serve melon wedges or another fresh fruit, almond curd with mandarin oranges, or a refreshing sherbet.

Keep your menu simple at first. With a little practice your expertise and your confidence will increase, and soon you will be preparing meals fit for an emperor.

The Chinese Tea Lunch

Yum cha, or "tea lunch," is a treat for the entire family. Many Chinese families reserve Sunday mornings for this outing. It is not only an opportunity to savor the delights of *deem sum,* but to visit with friends as well. Afterward, a leisurely stroll around Chinatown dispels any feelings of overindulgence. Perhaps you have a teahouse nearby, but have been reluctant to experiment without guidance. Let me introduce you to *yum cha.*

The Chinese call the little delicacies served at tea lunch *deem sum,* which translates as "touching your heart." And that indeed is what these small morsels do. The advantage of sampling them at a teahouse is the great variety available. It may take you several visits to determine your favorites. There are steamed shrimp and pork dumplings, deep-fried egg rolls and taro-root dumplings, green peppers with shrimp filling, and on and on. Some teahouses have two dozen varieties. Later you can make one or two at home. Most of the recipes in the Appetizers chapter are served as *deem sum*.

The first step in *yum cha* is the selection of your tea. The waiter will ask you for your choice, and you might take this opportunity to try a variety you haven't tasted before. For the uninitiated, I would suggest the mild *po nay,* but *loong jaing* (dragon's well), *look on* (six virtues), or jasmine are some of the other alternatives. When your teapot is empty, turn the lid of the teapot on its side or upside down. This is the universal signal to the waiter that it is time for a refill.

Now the fun begins. There is no need to ask for a menu (although there usually is one listing soups and noodle and clay-pot dishes). The food will come to you on carts or on trays. Some items are on plates, some in metal or bamboo steamers; each serving contains 2 to 6 pieces, depending on the item. If you see something that interests you, just point.

There are four main groups of food from which to choose. The first is made up of steamed dishes like half-moon dumplings, pork buns, and shrimp or pork dumplings. The second group is the *lo mei,* or "variety group," such as parchment chicken, pickled mustard greens, black-bean spareribs, and duck feet. The third classification covers deep-fried items: egg rolls, rice rolls, pork triangles, and the like. The fourth group is comprised of sweet items like sugar gelatin cake, sponge cake, Chinese doughnuts, and delightful custard tarts. You may also order won ton soup, chow mein, and *chow fun* (stir-fried rice noodles). In the larger restaurants, you will see rice casseroles containing chicken, pork, and mushrooms. The manner in which they are cooked imparts to the rice the flavors of the various ingredients, making for a truly delicious dish.

Most of the larger teahouses have now adopted the Hong Kong system of stamping a mark on your bill for each dish you select. Then it becomes a simple matter for the waiter to count the number of marks to calculate your check. You may, however, encounter small teahouses that still use the time-honored custom of counting the steamers and plates on your table to reckon the bill.

Most teahouses are open every day, and tea lunch is served from about 8:00 A.M. to 3:00 P.M. Some of the more special items might not be available in the afternoon, however. Regardless of the teahouse you visit, I'm sure you will enjoy the experience of authentic *yum cha*.

APPETIZERS

CHINESE DOUGHNUTS
(Jeen Dui)

3 oz. brown sugar bars
1 c. plus 2 tbsp. cold water
1 recipe Pork and Shrimp or Sweet
  Filling (following)
1 lb. (3 c.) glutinous rice flour
2 tbsp. sugar
¼ c. raw white sesame seeds
1½ qt. oil for deep-frying

Makes about 16

1. Dissolve sugar bars by placing them in the water overnight.
2. Make filling of choice and set aside.
3. Put the glutinous rice flour and granulated sugar in a mixing bowl. Stir to combine. Add dissolved brown sugar and mix well. Turn the dough out onto a lightly floured pastry board and knead it with your hands until it has the consistency of chocolate-chip cookie dough.
4. Divide dough into 3 or 4 portions. Roll 1 portion into a rope about 2″ in diameter. To do this, rest the dough under your palm and move your hand back and forth in a steady motion. As the dough begins to lengthen, use 2 hands, continuing in the same manner. When the rope is the proper diameter, cut it into 1½″ pieces with a damp towel until ready to use. Roll and cut remaining dough in the same manner.
5. Shape each 1½″ piece into a ball about 2½″ in diameter. Make a deep indentation in the center of the ball with your fingertips.
6. Put ¾ tbsp. filling into each indentation and bring up the sides of the dough to enclose the filling. Twist the dough where it meets at the top. Be sure it is twisted tight so that the doughnut doesn't fall apart during deep-frying.
7. Put the sesame seeds on a plate and lightly roll each doughnut in them to coat the exterior.
8. Heat oil in wok to 325 degrees. Gently drop in a few doughnuts at a time. Keep them separated, as they are apt to stick together.
9. When the doughnuts begin to brown and float (about 2 minutes), gently press ("bounce") each one into the oil several times with your Chinese strainer. This makes the doughnut puffy. Fry for 3 minutes longer on each side (6 minutes total cooking time).
10. Remove and drain on paper towels. Cook remaining doughnuts in the same manner. Serve hot.

Advance preparation: Step 1 must be done in advance. Steps 2 and 3 can be done a few hours ahead and kept at room temperature.

Variation: The doughnuts may be made without filling. Shape the dough into balls about 1″ in diameter or into "cigar" shapes about 1½″ by ½″. Fry as above.

Note: These doughnuts are a favorite pastry of the Chinese. They are delicious when eaten freshly cooked and are usually enjoyed during the Chinese New Year's celebration.

SWEET FILLING FOR DOUGHNUTS
(Tim Jeen Dui)

1. If using raw peanuts, toast them in a 325-degree oven until golden brown (about 15 minutes). When cool, chop fine.
2. Toast sesame seeds in a dry (no oil) frying pan over medium heat until golden brown (about 1 minute).
3. Dice candied winter melon into ¼" pieces.
4. Combine peanuts, sesame seeds, candied melon, and coconut. Mix well.

Advance preparation: The peanuts and sesame seeds may be toasted (steps 1 and 2) up to 2 weeks in advance and stored together in an airtight container at room temperature. Step 3 may be completed a few days in advance and stored in a separate container at room temperature.

Note: As with the pork and shrimp filling, you may find you have a little more filling than you need for the doughnuts. This mixture is great snack food.

⅔ c. raw peanuts or unsalted roasted
   peanuts
⅓ c. raw white sesame seeds
2 oz. candied winter melon
½ c. sweetened shredded coconut

For 16 doughnuts

PORK AND SHRIMP FILLING FOR DOUGHNUTS
(Ha Yuk Jeen Dui)

1. Place pork in a bowl. Add seasoning ingredients and mix well.
2. Boil mushrooms in water to cover for 10 minutes. Drain, rinse, and squeeze dry. Cut off and discard stems. Chop into very small pieces.
3. Shell, devein, wash, and drain prawns. Dice the prawns fine.
4. Heat wok and add oil. Add pork and mushrooms and stir-fry for 2 minutes over high heat.
5. Add chicken stock, cover, and cook for 3 minutes over medium-high heat.
6. Add prawns, green onion, and jicama.
7. Stir in thickener. Cook for 30 seconds. Let cool before using.

Advance preparation: The entire recipe may be made a day in advance and refrigerated.

Note: You may end up with some extra filling. It can be added to fried rice or eaten as a small snack.

½ lb. ground lean pork
10 small Chinese dried black
   mushrooms
¼ lb. medium-sized prawns in the shell
2 tbsp. oil
½ c. chicken stock
1 green onion, chopped
¼ c. finely chopped jicama

Seasoning:

½ tsp. salt
½ tsp. sugar
½ tsp. thin soy sauce
½ tsp. oyster sauce
1 tsp. cornstarch

Thickener:

1 tbsp. cornstarch, mixed well with
   1 tbsp. cold water

For 16 doughnuts

CHINESE FRIED DUMPLINGS
(Jow Gwok Jai)

½ c. raw or unsalted roasted peanuts
¼ c. raw white sesame seeds
4 slices candied winter melon*
¾ c. sweetened shredded coconut
1 package (1 lb.) round dumpling
   skins**
3 c. oil for deep-frying

Sealing Mixture:

1 tbsp. all-purpose flour, mixed with 2
   tbsp. cold water

*Candied winter melon can be purchased in Chinese groceries, gift shops, and bakeries. Candied pear or pineapple may be substituted. They can be found in natural-foods stores.

**Dumpling skins are similar to won ton skins except that they are slightly thinner and are round. You may substitute won ton skins; fold the dumplings into a triangle rather than a half-moon shape or trim off the corners of the skins before folding to make them round.

Makes about 80

1. If using raw peanuts, toast them in a 325-degree oven until golden brown (about 15 minutes). When cool, chop fine.
2. Toast sesame seeds in a dry (no oil) frying pan over medium heat until golden brown (about 1 minute).
3. Dice candied winter melon into ¼″ pieces.
4. Combine peanuts, sesame seeds, candied melon, and coconut. Mix well.
5. Place 1 tsp. of the filling mixture in the center of each dumpling skin. Moisten edge of skin with sealing mixture and fold in half to form a half-moon shape. Seal edges by pressing together firmly with your fingers.
6. Heat oil in wok to 325 degrees. Deep-fry dumplings, about 15 at a time, for 2 minutes. Turn and fry until a light golden brown (about 1 minute). Remove and drain on paper towels.
7. Repeat procedure with remaining dumplings. Serve hot or at room temperature.

Advance preparation: The peanuts and sesame seeds may be toasted (steps 1 and 2) up to 2 weeks in advance and stored together in an airtight container at room temperature.

Note: This is another popular food for the Chinese New Year's celebration. The dumplings will keep nicely in a closed container at room temperature for about 3 weeks.

EGG ROLLS
(Choon Guen)

1. Cut the pork, chicken, or ham, celery, onions, and bamboo shoots into thin julienne strips about 1″ long. (The bamboo shoots should measure ¾ c.) Place in a bowl.
2. Thinly slice mushrooms and add with bean sprouts to bowl containing other ingredients. Mix well.
3. Just before forming the egg rolls, add salt, sugar, soy sauce, and oyster sauce to meat and vegetables. Mix well.
4. Using about 2 rounded tbsp. filling per egg roll, wrap and seal egg rolls, following the directions in the accompanying diagram
5. Heat oil in wok to 325 degrees. Deep-fry egg rolls, about 8 at a time, for 3 minutes on each side (6 minutes total cooking time). Remove from oil and drain on paper towels. Serve hot.

Advance preparation: Egg rolls may be formed up to 2 hours in advance and stored in a closed container at room temperature. Separate layers with waxed paper to prevent them from sticking together. (Egg rolls stacked this way may be frozen and then transferred to plastic bags and placed in the freezer for up to 2 months; deep-fry without defrosting.) They may also be deep-fried several hours in advance, then placed in an uncovered pan and reheated in a preheated 375-degree oven for 10 minutes.

Note: Any extra filling can be mixed into fried rice or tossed with noodles.

Serving suggestions: Catsup, hot mustard, and/or Worcestershire sauce are good condiments. These egg rolls make delightful hors d'oeuvres. You may wish to cut them into thirds or halves on the diagonal for easier handling.

½ lb. barbecued pork or cooked chicken or ham
2 stalks celery
2 green onions
½ can (15 oz.) whole winter bamboo shoots
¼ lb. fresh mushrooms
¼ lb. bean sprouts
½ tsp. salt
½ tsp. sugar
1 tsp. thin soy sauce
1½ tbsp. oyster sauce
1 package (1 lb.) egg roll skins*
1 qt. oil for deep-frying

Sealing Mixture:

1 tbsp. all-purpose flour, mixed with 2 tbsp. cold water

*This recipe requires very thin egg roll skins, such as those sold under the brand names Doll, Ho Tai, Menlo, or Chinese Inn. Carefully separate and then loosely restack the skins before you begin to fill the egg rolls. This will make the forming of the rolls go more quickly and easily. (You may separate the skins several hours in advance, loosely restack, wrap in foil, and refrigerate until ready to use.)

Makes 25

HOW TO WRAP AN EGG ROLL

1. Place the skin with one corner pointing toward you. Place about 2 tbsp. filling about 2″ in from the corner.
2. Fold the corner nearest you over to just cover the filling.
3. Fold over again about 1¼″ (you should now have a triangle), leaving at least 2½″ at the top, as shown.
4. Fold the right and then the left corners toward the center, like an envelope; the "package" should be about 4″ long.
5. Roll tightly from the side nearest you to form a cylinder.
6. Moisten the open corner with sealing mixture. Fold it toward you, pressing firmly.

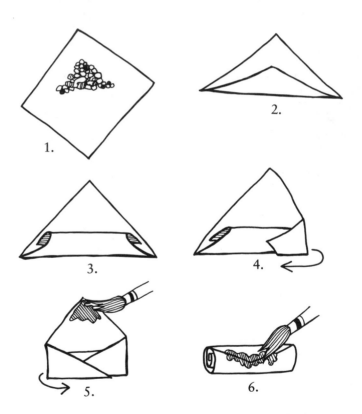

PARCHMENT CHICKEN
(Gee Bow Gai)

1. Skin and bone chicken. Cut into 1½" by ½" pieces. Place in a bowl.
2. Add cornstarch to chicken and mix well. Add marinade ingredients and mix well again. Toss in onions and ginger. Marinate at room temperature for 2 hours.
3. Wrap and seal chicken pieces in egg roll skins, following directions in accompanying diagram.
4. Heat oil in wok to 325 degrees. Deep-fry packages, about 8 at a time, for 2 minutes on each side (4 minutes total cooking time). Remove to paper towels to drain. Serve hot.

Advance preparation: Parchment chicken may be deep-fried several hours in advance and reheated in an uncovered pan in a preheated 325-degree oven for 10 minutes just before serving.

Note: You may use 5" squares of aluminum foil in place of the egg roll skins. (The flavor of the chicken will be the same, but you won't have the delightful "crunch" of the skin, and you will, of course, have to unwrap the chicken before eating it. That can also be fun, however.) To wrap in foil, place foil square with one corner pointing toward you. Place a chicken piece in the center and fold foil in half toward you to make a triangle. Fold one open edge over the center about ¼", fold again, and pinch edges together. Repeat with other open edge.

Foil-wrapped chicken may be deep-fried as above, or roasted in a preheated 400-degree oven for about 30 minutes. Check a piece of chicken after that time to make sure it is cooked. If not, give the packages a little more time.

1 whole chicken (about 3½ lb.)
1 tbsp. cornstarch
3 green onions, finely chopped
1 tbsp. finely chopped ginger
1 package (1 lb.) egg roll skins*
1 qt. oil for deep-frying

Marinade:

1 tbsp. catsup
1 tbsp. oyster sauce
1½ tbsp. hoisin sauce
1 tsp. thin soy sauce
1 tbsp. white wine
dash of pepper
1 tsp. salt
1 tsp. sugar

Sealing Mixture:

1 tbsp. all-purpose flour, mixed with 2 tbsp. cold water

*This recipe requires very thin egg roll skins. See comments on these skins on recipe for Egg Rolls.

Makes about 25

How to Wrap Parchment Chicken

1. Position the skin with one corner pointing toward you. Place 1 piece of chicken about 2″ in from that corner.
2. Fold the corner nearest you over to just cover the chicken.
3. Fold over again about 1¼″ (you should now have a triangle), leaving at least 2½″ at the top, as shown.
4. Fold the right and then the left corners toward the center, like an envelope; the "package" should be about 4″ long.
5. Moisten the remaining corner with the sealing mixture and fold down like the flap of an envelope, pressing firmly to seal.

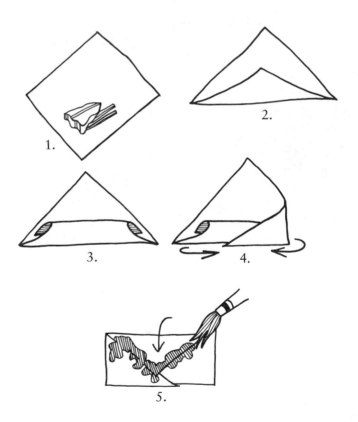

POT STICKERS
(Huo Tip)

1. Chop cabbage fine. You should have about 1 c.
2. Put pork, green onions, ginger, and preserved vegetables on a chopping board. Chop and mix with a cleaver until minced and well blended, about 1 minute. (This step may be done in a food processor.) Place in a bowl.
3. Add seasoning ingredients, cabbage, and egg to pork mixture. Mix well.
4. Wrap and seal pork mixture in pot sticker skins, following directions in accompanying diagram.
5. Combine ingredients for dipping mixture and set aside.
6. Heat a large frying pan. Add 2 tbsp. oil and half of the pot stickers. Pan-fry over high heat, on the base side only, until lightly browned (about 30 seconds).
7. Add 1⅓ c. chicken stock, cover, and cook over high heat until most of the chicken stock is absorbed, approximately 7 minutes. Then brown pot stickers again until the skin is crisp (watch carefully to be sure they don't burn!). Remove to platter and keep warm.
8. Repeat steps 6 and 7 with remaining uncooked pot stickers, oil, and chicken stock. Serve immediately with dipping mixture.

Advance preparation: Pot stickers may be formed a few hours in advance of cooking, covered, and refrigerated. Uncooked pot stickers may be frozen for up to 3 months. Freeze, well separated, on a baking sheet, then store in an airtight container or plastic bag. Do not defrost before cooking, but increase cooking time slightly.

4 oz. cabbage
1¼ lb. ground lean pork
2 green onions, chopped
2 tsp. finely chopped ginger root
2 tbsp. Tientsin preserved vegetables, rinsed and chopped
1 large egg, beaten
1 package (1 lb.) pot sticker skins
4 tbsp. oil
2⅔ c. chicken stock

Seasoning:

¾ tsp. salt
¾ tsp. sugar
2 tsp. thin soy sauce
1 tbsp. oyster sauce
1½ tbsp. white wine
2 tbsp. cornstarch

Sealing Mixture:

1 tbsp. all-purpose flour, mixed with 2 tbsp. cold water

Dipping Mixture:

3 tbsp. thin soy sauce
1½ tbsp. Hot Spiced Oil (following)
1½ tbsp. white vinegar

Makes about 35

How to Wrap a Pot Sticker

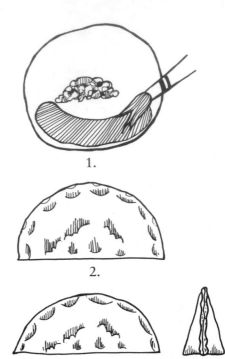

1. Spoon ¾ tbsp. filling in center of a pot sticker skin. Brush edges lightly with sealing mixture.
2. Fold skin in half. Press edges of skin together with fingers, being careful not to squeeze filling. Flute sealed edges with your fingers (as you would pie crust).
3. Grasp pot sticker along its side and gently press base on a flat surface, flattening the pot sticker so it will stand on its bottom. (The flatter they are, the less chicken stock you will need when you cook them.)

Hot Spiced Oil
(Laht Yau)

1 c. safflower oil
2 tbsp. crushed dried red chili pepper

Makes 1 c.

1. Heat oil in a small saucepan over medium heat for 2 minutes.
2. To test oil temperature, drop in a pinch of chili pepper. If it turns brown, add remaining chili pepper. If it turns black, let oil cool 1–2 minutes and test again.
3. Remove oil from heat. Let cool. Pour into a jar and let stand for 1 week before using. The red chili pepper will settle to the bottom and need not be removed.

Note: This oil will keep for several months at room temperature. It is used as a condiment, with or without soy sauce, for dumplings, stir-fried rice noodles, and chow mein.

SHRIMP BALLS
(Ha Kau)

1. Crumble bread and soak in the water.
2. Shell, devein, wash, and drain prawns.
3. If using fresh water chestnuts, peel and remove and discard the top and root ends. Crush fresh or canned water chestnuts with the flat side of the cleaver, or chop fine.
4. Place prawns, bacon, onion, and water chestnuts or jicama on a chopping board. Chop and mix with a cleaver until minced and well blended, about 1 minute. (This step may be done in a food processor.) Place in a bowl.
5. Add seasoning ingredients to prawn mixture and mix well. Add the soaked bread and mix again.
6. Form prawn mixture into balls about 1¼″ in diameter.
7. Heat oil in wok to 325 degrees. Deep-fry shrimp balls, about 12 at a time, for 2 minutes on each side (4 minutes total cooking time). Remove and drain on paper towels. Serve hot.

Advance preparation: Steps 1–6 may be done the day before and refrigerated.

Note: Shrimp balls may be pan-fried by flattening into patties about 2″ in diameter and ¼″ thick. Fry 6 or 7 at a time in a small amount of oil until they are golden brown (about 2 minutes on each side).

1 slice white bread
2 tbsp. cold water
1 lb. medium-sized prawns in the shell
6 fresh or canned water chestnuts, or
   ¼ c. finely chopped jicama
2 slices bacon, finely chopped
   (optional)*
1 green onion, chopped
3 c. oil for deep-frying

Seasoning:

1 tsp. salt
½ tsp. sugar
½ tsp. thin soy sauce
1 tsp. oyster sauce
1 small egg
2 tbsp. cornstarch

*The bacon is optional, but gives the shrimp balls very good flavor.

Makes about 36

SHRIMP CAKES
(Ha Behng)

1 lb. meduim-sized prawns in the shell
1/3 c. finely chopped jicama
1 green onion, finely chopped
1/3 c. finely chopped barbecued pork or
   cooked ham
1/3 c. oil for pan-frying

Seasoning:

1/2 tsp. salt
1 tsp. sugar
1 tsp. thin soy sauce
2 tsp. oyster sauce
1 small egg
2 tbsp. cornstarch

Condiment:

1/4 c. sweet chili sauce

Makes about 20

1. Shell, devein, wash, and drain prawns.
2. Place prawns, jicama, green onion, and barbecued pork on a chopping board. Chop and mix with a cleaver until they are minced and well blended, about 1 minute. (This step may be done in a food processor.) Place in a bowl.
3. Add seasoning ingredients to prawn mixture. Mix well.
4. Flatten prawn mixture into patties about 2" in diameter and 1/4" thick. There should be approximately 20 patties.
5. Heat a frying pan (preferably with a nonstick coating). Add 3 tbsp. oil and fry 7 or 8 patties at a time for 2 minutes. Remove and keep warm.
6. Repeat procedure with remaining prawn mixture and oil. Serve with chili sauce.

Advance preparation: Steps 1–4 may be done the day before and refrigerated.

Serving suggestions: Shrimp cakes make excellent hors d'oeuvres. Serve with sweet chili sauce as suggested, or with Sweet-and-Sour Dipping Sauce (see Noodles, Won Tons, and Rice chapter).

SHRIMP TOAST
(Ha Doh See)

1. Shell, devein, wash, and drain prawns.
2. Mince prawns. Place in a bowl.
3. Add egg white, green onion, red or yellow onion, and seasoning ingredients to prawns. Mix well.
4. Toast bread lightly. Remove crusts. Cut each slice into 4 triangles by making 2 diagonal cuts.
5. Spread each toast triangle generously with shrimp mixture.
6. Heat a frying pan (preferably with a nonstick coating). Add 2 tbsp. oil and half the shrimp triangles, shrimp side down. Fry for 2 minutes over medium heat. Turn and fry second side for 1 minute. Remove and keep warm.
7. Repeat with remaining oil and shrimp triangles. Serve hot.

Advance preparation: The shrimp mixture may be prepared up to a day ahead and refrigerated. The toast can be spread with the shrimp mixture an hour before pan-frying. You may also pan-fry the triangles in advance, reducing the cooking time of the shrimp side to 1 minute and the opposite side to 30 seconds. Reheat them in a preheated 350-degree oven for 8 minutes just before serving.

½ lb. medium-sized prawns in the shell
egg white from 1 small egg, beaten
1 small green onion, finely chopped
2 tbsp. finely chopped yellow or red onion
4–5 slices white bread
4 tbsp. oil

Seasoning:

¼ tsp. salt
¼ tsp. sugar
¼ tsp. thin soy sauce
dash of pepper
1½ tbsp. cornstarch

Serves 4–6

SOUPS

BASIC RICE SOUP

(Jook or Congee)

1¼ c. long-grain white rice
¾ tsp. salt
1 tbsp. oil
3 qt. chicken stock
½ c. raw peanuts (optional)
1 recipe Beef, Chicken, or Pork
   Meatballs for Rice Soup (following)
2 green onions, finely chopped
1 tbsp. slivered ginger

Serves 6–8

1. Wash rice in 4 changes of water and drain well. Place in a bowl and add salt and oil. Let stand at room temperature overnight. (This standing time makes the rice very smooth; the time may be reduced if necessary.)
2. Bring chicken stock to a boil.
3. Add rice and peanuts. Bring to a boil again, cover, and cook over medium heat for 2 hours. Stir frequently so that the rice does not burn. The soup should have the consistency of oatmeal mush mixed with milk.
4. While soup cooks, prepare the beef, chicken, or pork meatballs.
5. Taste soup and adjust with salt.
6. Add beef, chicken, or pork meatballs. Cover and cook for 10 minutes.
7. Garnish with onions and ginger.

Advance preparation: Steps 1–4 may be completed several days in advance and refrigerated. Bring to a boil before adding meat.

Note: The Chinese often eat this hearty soup for breakfast or a late-night snack.

BEEF FOR RICE SOUP

(Ngow Yuk Jook)

1 lb. flank steak

Seasoning:

1 tsp. salt
½ tsp. sugar
1 tsp. oyster sauce
1 tsp. thin soy sauce
2 tsp. white wine
1 tbsp. cornstarch

1. Cut flank steak lengthwise (with grain of meat) into 3 equal strips each about 1½″ wide. Cut each strip across the grain into thin slices. Place in a bowl.
2. Add seasoning ingredients to beef. Mix well.

Advance preparation: The entire recipe may be prepared 1 day in advance and refrigerated.

CHICKEN FOR RICE SOUP

(Gai Jook)

1. Skin and bone chicken. Cut meat into pieces 1½″ by ½″. Place in a bowl.
2. Add seasoning ingredients to chicken. Mix well.

Advance preparation: The entire recipe may be prepared 1 day in advance and refrigerated.

2 whole chicken breasts

Seasoning:

¾ tsp. salt
½ tsp. sugar
dash of pepper
1½ tsp. thin soy sauce
1 tbsp. cornstarch

PORK MEATBALLS FOR RICE SOUP

(Yuk Kau Jook)

1. Shell, devein, wash, and drain prawns.
2. Chop prawns very fine. Place in a bowl with pork and green onion.
3. Add seasoning ingredients to pork mixture. Mix well.
4. Form into balls about 1″ in diameter.

Advance preparation: The entire recipe may be prepared 1 day in advance and refrigerated.

¼ lb. medium-sized prawns in the shell
¾ lb. ground lean pork
1 green onion, finely chopped

Seasoning:

1 tsp. salt
½ tsp. sugar
1 tsp. thin soy sauce
2 tbsp. cornstarch

CHICKEN CORN SOUP

(Sook Mai Gai Tong)

1 whole chicken breast, or 1 lb. chicken
   thighs
¼ lb. fresh mushrooms
2 tbsp. oil
1 qt. chicken stock
1 can (8 oz.) creamed corn
2 large eggs, lightly beaten
1 green onion, finely chopped
¼ c. finely chopped cooked ham

Seasoning:

½ tsp. salt
½ tsp. sugar
1 tsp. thin soy sauce
2 tsp. white wine
2 tsp. cornstarch

Thickener:

2 tbsp. cornstarch, mixed well with
   3 tbsp. cold water
2 tsp. dark soy sauce
1 tbsp. sesame oil

Serves 5

1. Skin and bone chicken. Mince meat with a cleaver. It should have the texture of ground beef. (A food processor may be used for this step.) Place in a bowl.
2. Add seasoning ingredients to the chicken. Mix well.
3. Finely chop mushrooms.
4. Combine thickener ingredients and set aside.
5. Heat wok and add oil. Add chicken and stir-fry for 1 minute over high heat, breaking the meat apart as it cooks.
6. Add chicken stock, creamed corn, and mushrooms. Bring to a boil, cover, and cook for 1 minute.
7. Stir in thickener. Cook for 30 seconds.
8. Stir beaten eggs into soup in a circular motion. Immediately turn off heat. Garnish with green onion and ham. Serve.

Advance preparation: Steps 1–6 may be done a few hours ahead and kept at room temperature.

CHICKEN MEATBALL SOUP

(Gai Kau Tong)

1. Skin and bone chicken. Mince chicken meat with a cleaver. (A food processor may be used for this step.) You should have about ¾ c. Place in a bowl.
2. Add seasoning ingredients to chicken. Mix well.
3. Form chicken mixture into balls approximately 1¼" in diameter. (This amount should make about 14.)
4. Bring chicken stock to a boil in wok. Add chicken meatballs, cover, and cook for 2 minutes over high heat.
5. Add peas and cook for 1 minute.
6. Stir beaten egg into soup in a circular motion. Serve immediately.

Advance preparation: Steps 1–3 may be completed a few hours in advance and kept at room temperature.

Variation: This recipe can be varied by using ¾ c. ground lean pork or minced prawns in place of the chicken.

½ lb. chicken breast
1 qt. chicken stock
¾ c. fresh or defrosted frozen peas
1 egg, lightly beaten

Seasoning:

½ tsp. salt
½ tsp. sugar
½ tsp. thin soy sauce
1 tsp. cornstarch
dash of pepper

Serves 4

CHICKEN WHISKEY SOUP
(Gai Jau Tong)

1 whole chicken breast
4 dried red dates
10 small Chinese black dried
    mushrooms
14 dried lily flowers
4 pieces dried black fungus
1 tbsp. oil
5 c. chicken stock
1 tbsp. slivered ginger root
2 tbsp. whiskey

Seasoning:

1/2 tsp. salt
1/2 tsp. sugar
1/2 tsp. thin soy sauce
dash of pepper

Serves 4

1. Skin and bone chicken. Cut into pieces 1½" by ½". Place in a bowl.
2. Add seasoning ingredients to chicken. Mix well.
3. Soak red dates, mushrooms, lily flowers, and fungus in warm water to cover for 15 minutes. Drain, rinse well, and drain again.
4. Remove and discard date seeds. Cut dates into small pieces.
5. Squeeze moisture from mushrooms. Remove and discard stems. Cut mushrooms into strips, julienne style.
6. Cut ½" from pointed end of each lily flower and discard. Cut each flower in half crosswise.
7. Remove and discard stems of fungus. Cut into 1" slivers; they should measure about ¾ c.
8. Heat wok and add oil. Add chicken and stir-fry for 2 minutes over high heat.
9. Add chicken stock, ginger, whiskey, and all presoaked ingredients. Bring to a boil, cover, and simmer over medium heat for 15 minutes. Serve.

Advance preparation: This recipe may be completed 1 week in advance and reheated before serving.

Note: By tradition, this soup, along with Pigs' Feet in Vinegar Sauce (see Meats chapter), is served to new mothers for a full month after the birth of a baby, to help them regain their strength and vigor. These two dishes are also offered to any visitors who come to see the new infant during this period. Since rather large quantities are required to fulfill these needs, both dishes are made in big batches.

EGG FLOWER SOUP
(Gai Don Tong)

1. Chop flank steak with a cleaver until it is the consistency of ground beef. (This step may be done in a food processor.) Place in a bowl.
2. Add seasoning ingredients to beef. Mix well.
3. If using snow peas, remove tips. Finely sliver the snow peas.
4. Combine thickener ingredients and set aside.
5. Bring chicken stock to a boil.
6. Add beef and stir to separate meat into small pieces. Add peas. Cover and cook for 2 minutes.
7. Stir in thickener. Cook for 30 seconds.
8. Stir beaten eggs into soup in a circular motion. Immediately turn off heat.
9. Garnish with green onion and serve at once.

Advance preparation: Steps 1–5 may be completed a few hours in advance and kept at room temperature. Reheat and proceed from step 6.

½ lb. flank steak
½ c. fresh or defrosted frozen peas, or
   15 snow peas
1 qt. chicken stock
2 eggs, lightly beaten
1 green onion, finely chopped

Seasoning:

¼ tsp. salt
¼ tsp. sugar
1 tsp. thin soy sauce
1 tsp. cornstarch

Thickener:

1 tbsp. cornstarch, mixed well with 1
   tbsp. cold water
2 tsp. dark soy sauce
1 tsp. sesame oil

Serves 4

HOT-AND-SOUR SOUP
(Sheun Lot Tong)

1 whole chicken breast
3 pieces dried black fungus
6 oz. fresh firm bean cake*
1 qt. chicken stock
½ c. shredded canned winter bamboo
  shoots
2 eggs, lightly beaten
1½ tbsp. white vinegar
¼ tsp. pepper

Seasoning:

¼ tsp. salt
¼ tsp. sugar
¾ tsp. thin soy sauce
1 tsp. cornstarch
dash of pepper

Thickener:

1½ tbsp. cornstarch, mixed well with 3
  tbsp. cold water
1½ tbsp. dark soy sauce

*Be sure to buy firm bean cake. The
soft variety will fall apart if prepared in
this way. See Ingredients for Chinese
Cooking for additional information on
fresh bean cake.

Serves 4

1. Skin and bone chicken. Cut meat into thin strips, julienne style. Place in a bowl.
2. Add seasoning ingredients to chicken. Mix well.
3. Soak fungus in warm water to cover for 15 minutes. Drain, rinse thoroughly, and drain again. Remove and discard stems. Cut into 1″ slivers; you should have about ½ c.
4. Cut bean cake into slices 1″ long by ¼″ thick.
5. Bring chicken stock to a boil. Add chicken, black fungus, and bamboo shoots. Cover and cook for 3 minutes.
6. Add bean cake. Bring quickly to a boil (do not overcook!).
7. Stir in thickener. Cook for 30 seconds.
8. Stir beaten egg into soup in a circular motion. Immediately turn off heat. Adjust seasoning with salt.
9. Add vinegar and pepper. Mix well and serve. (Some people like more vinegar or pepper, so add them to suit your taste.)

Advance preparation: This soup may be completed through step 5 a few days in advance and refrigerated. Steps 6–9 should be done immediately before serving.

SEAWEED SOUP
(Gee Choy Tong)

1. Cut pork or chicken into pieces 1½" by 1". Place in a bowl.
2. Add seasoning ingredients to meat. Mix well.
3. Cut Napa cabbage into pieces 1" wide.
4. Break seaweed into 3" squares. Rinse briefly under running water.
5. Bring chicken stock to a boil. Add pork and seaweed. Reduce the heat, cover, and cook over medium heat for 5 minutes.
6. Add Napa cabbage. Bring to a boil and serve.

Advance preparation: Steps 1–5 may be completed a few hours ahead and kept at room temperature.

½ lb. lean pork or boned and skinned chicken meat
¼ lb. Napa cabbage
3 sheets dried seaweed
5 c. chicken stock

Seasoning:

½ tsp. salt
½ tsp. sugar
½ tsp. thin soy sauce
1 tsp. cornstarch

Serves 5

Sizzling Rice Soup

(Woh Bay Tong)

2 c. hot cooked short-grain white rice*
¼ lb. medium-sized prawns in the shell
½ lb. Napa cabbage
1½ c. oil for deep-frying
1 qt. chicken stock
½ c. fresh or defrosted frozen peas

Seasoning:

½ tsp. salt
½ tsp. sugar
½ tsp. thin soy sauce
1 tsp. cornstarch
dash of pepper

*Short-grain rice is stickier than long-grain rice, so it makes a better patty. It is, however, cooked in the same way. (See recipe for Steamed Rice in Noodles, Won Tons, and Rice chapter.)

Serves 4

1. Press hot cooked rice into a thin layer (no more than ¼″ thick) on a baking sheet. Place in a preheated 300-degree oven for 30 minutes. Remove from the oven, turn the rice layer over (this will be easy to do as the rice will have firmed up), and return it to the oven for an additional 30 minutes. Remove from the oven, and when cool enough to handle, break into 3″ pieces.
2. Shell, devein, wash, and drain prawns.
3. Dice prawns and place in a bowl. Add seasoning ingredients to prawns. Mix well.
4. Cut Napa cabbage into pieces 1″ wide.
5. Heat oil in wok to 325 degrees.
6. Meanwhile, bring chicken stock to a boil. Add prawns, peas, and Napa cabbage. Return to a boil.
7. Deep-fry rice patties until golden brown (about 5 minutes). Remove and drain on paper towels.
8. Pour the hot soup into a deep serving bowl and immediately add the rice patties. Both the rice patties and the soup must be as hot as possible to produce the sizzle. If the timing isn't perfect, the soup may be reheated but the rice patties cannot. (This final step, which is quite showy, may be done at the table.) Serve at once.

Advance preparation: Rice patties may be baked 2 weeks in advance, stored in an airtight container, and refrigerated. They may also be frozen for up to 2 months.

Serving suggestion: This soup goes well with Mongolian Beef and Curried Chicken.

WINTER MELON SOUP
(Doong Gwah Tong)

1. Skin and bone chicken. Cut meat into ½" cubes. Place in a bowl.
2. Add seasoning ingredients to chicken. Mix well.
3. Remove skin from winter melon. Cut pulp into ½" cubes.
4. Bring chicken stock to a boil. Add winter melon and chicken cubes. Cover and cook for 10 minutes over high heat.
5. Add jicama and mushrooms. Cover and cook for 2 minutes over high heat.
6. Stir in thickener. Cook for 30 seconds. Serve.

Advance preparation: The entire recipe may be completed several hours ahead and kept at room temperature. Reheat just before serving.

Note: This is a simplified winter melon soup. The traditional soup is made by simmering all of the ingredients in a whole winter melon for 3 to 4 hours. The resulting dish is a flavorful blend of the melon essence and the vegetables and meat.

*1 lb. chicken thighs, or 1 whole
 chicken breast*
½ lb. winter melon
5 c. chicken stock
1 c. cubed (½") jicama
½ c. sliced fresh or canned mushrooms

Seasoning:

1 tsp. salt
½ tsp. sugar
½ tsp. thin soy sauce
1 tsp. cornstarch

Thickener:

*1 tbsp. cornstarch, mixed well with 2
 tbsp. cold water*
1 tsp. dark soy sauce

Serves 5

POULTRY

CANTONESE BOILED CHICKEN
(Bok Cheet Gai)

3-3½ lb. chicken
4 qt. water
2 tsp. salt
1 slice ginger root (about ½" thick and
   1" in diameter), peeled and crushed
1 whole green onion
2 green onions, slivered

Condiments:

oyster sauce
2 tbsp. mustard powder, mixed with 2
   tbsp. cold water

Serves 8

1. Rinse chicken and remove any pin feathers.
2. Bring water and salt to a boil in a large pot.
3. Add ginger, whole green onion, and chicken, on its back, to the pot. Immediately turn heat to very low. Simmer in this position for 15 minutes. Turn bird onto its breast side and simmer 15 minutes more. Simmer an additional 15 minutes on each side (1 hour total cooking time). Turning the chicken assures that all parts will be cooked.
4. Remove the chicken from the pot to a colander. Place under cold running water for 2 minutes. Remove and let cool to room temperature.
5. Chop chicken into serving pieces. To do this, separate drumsticks and thighs from bird and cut each crosswise into 3 pieces. Cut each wing into 2 pieces. Separate back from breast and split each in half lengthwise. Cut each section crosswise into 6 pieces. Arrange pieces on a serving platter.
6. Garnish with slivered green onions. Serve at room temperature with hot mustard and oyster sauce.

Advance preparation: This dish may be prepared a few hours in advance and kept at room temperature.

Variations: To vary this recipe for company, arrange the chopped chicken neatly in the center of a large platter and surround it with one of the following vegetables.

With Bok Choy:

1. Break branches off center stalk of 1 lb. bok choy. Remove and discard any flowers.
2. Peel outer covering off center stalk. Cut stalk on the diagonal into 2" pieces.
3. Trim stem end off each leaf where it was attached to the stalk. Cut stems and leaves into 2" lengths.
4. Heat wok and add 1 tbsp. oil. Add bok choy and stir-fry for 2 minutes over high heat, adding ¾ tsp. each salt and sugar.
5. Add ½ c. chicken stock (from boiling the chicken) and 1 tsp. dark soy sauce. Bring to a boil.
6. Mix together 1 tbsp. cornstarch and 2 tbsp. cold water. Add to bok choy and cook for 1 minute more.
7. Arrange the bok choy around the cold chicken. Serve.

With Snow Peas:

1. Remove tips from 30 snow peas. Cut on the diagonal into 2″ pieces.
2. Heat wok and add 1 tbsp. oil. Add snow peas and stir-fry for 1 minute over high heat, adding ¼ tsp. each salt and sugar.
3. Add ¼ c. chicken stock (from boiling the chicken) and ½ tsp. dark soy sauce. Bring to a boil.
4. Mix together 1 tsp. cornstarch and 2 tsp. cold water. Add to snow peas and cook for 30 seconds.
5. Arrange the snow peas around the cold chicken. Serve.

Note: Chinese housewives always prefer to buy fresh chickens, complete with head and feet, for this recipe. They especially enjoy the flavor and texture of the skin of the bird when it is prepared this way.

CANTONESE CHICKEN SALAD
(Sau See Gai)

2 whole chicken breasts, or 2 lb.
  chicken thighs
1½ c. cold water
⅓ c. raw peanuts or unsalted roasted
  peanuts
2 c. oil for deep-frying
1½ oz. rice sticks (py mei fun)
¼ c. raw white sesame seeds
15 snow peas (optional)
1 stalk celery
¼ head iceberg lettuce
1 tbsp. oil for stir-frying
1 green onion, slivered
salt and sugar

Seasoning:

½ tsp. salt
½ tsp. sugar
1 tsp. thin soy sauce
1 tsp. oyster sauce
⅛ tsp. five-spice powder

Spices for Salad:

½ tsp. dry mustard
1 tsp. cold water
1 tsp. sugar
¾ tsp. flavored salt*
1½ tbsp. oyster sauce
1½ tbsp. sesame oil
1 tsp. hoisin sauce

*To make flavored salt, heat 2 tbsp.
salt in a dry (no oil) frying pan for 2
minutes over medium heat. Remove
from the heat and stir in ⅛ tsp. five-
spice powder. Mix well. Any leftover
flavored salt will keep indefinitely if
stored in an airtight container.

Serves 6

1. Rub seasoning ingredients on the chicken.
2. Preheat oven to 375 degrees.
3. Pour water into a roasting pan. Put rack in the pan and arrange chicken pieces on rack. Roast, uncovered for 40 minutes, basting twice with the pan juices. (If the chicken hasn't browned after 15 minutes, increase the oven temperature to 400 degrees, or as needed.) Turn the chicken and roast an additional 30 minutes, again basting twice with pan juices (1 hour and 10 minutes total cooking time). Remove from the oven and let cool.
4. If using raw peanuts, toast in a 325-degree oven until golden brown (about 15 minutes).
5. Heat 2 c. oil in wok to 350 degrees. Drop rice sticks into hot oil. They will puff up within seconds. Remove with wire strainer and drain on paper towels.
6. Toast sesame seeds in a dry (no oil) frying pan over medium heat until golden brown (about 1 minute).
7. Remove tips from snow peas. Cut into strips, julienne style.
8. Peel celery. Cut into 1½"-long pieces. Cut each piece lengthwise into strips, julienne style.
9. Finely shred iceberg lettuce. You should have about 1 c.
10. Heat wok and add 1 tbsp. oil. Add snow peas, celery, and green onion and stir-fry for 2 minutes over high heat, sprinkling vegetables lightly with salt and sugar to taste. Do not overcook. Remove from wok and set aside.
11. Remove and discard skin from cooled chicken. Remove bones. Shred chicken meat by hand into a large bowl.
12. To make the salad spices, mix mustard with water. Add remaining ingredients and mix well. Add to chicken and toss until well mixed.
13. Add the stir-fried vegetables and lettuce. Mix well again.
14. Add the "crispies" (peanuts, sesame seeds, and rice sticks). Mix lightly and serve.

Advance preparation: The "crispies" (steps 4, 5, and 6) may be prepared 2 weeks in advance. They will retain their freshness if kept in closed containers at room temperature. The remaining steps through step 12 may be completed a few hours in advance and kept at room temperature.

Serving suggestion: This delicious salad makes a delightful light summer meal. Its charm and appeal is in the natural taste of the ingredients, which are not overpowered by a heavy dressing. It is ideal as a party dish or as a part of a multicourse dinner, since it requires no attention at the last minute.

Note: Chicken cooked this way is moist, juicy, and flavorful. Use it for any recipe calling for cooked chicken. The pan juices make a good gravy when thickened with a mixture of cornstarch and cold water.

CASHEW CHICKEN
(Yiu Gwoh Gai)

½ c. raw cashew nuts or unsalted
  roasted cashew nuts
1 whole chicken breast
1 stalk celery
½ yellow onion
1 carrot
¼ lb. fresh mushrooms
3 tbsp. oil
¼ tsp. salt
¼ tsp. sugar
1 c. chicken stock
¾ c. sliced winter bamboo shoots

Seasoning:

½ tsp. salt
½ tsp. sugar
1 tsp. thin soy sauce
1 tsp. oyster sauce
1 tbsp. cornstarch

Thickener:

1 tbsp. cornstarch, mixed well with 2
  tbsp. cold water
2 tsp. dark soy sauce
1 tbsp. sesame oil

Serves 4

1. If using raw cashews, roast in a 350-degree oven until golden brown (about 15 minutes).
2. Skin and bone chicken. Cut into ½″ cubes. Place in a bowl.
3. Add seasoning ingredients to chicken. Mix well.
4. Peel celery. Cut into 1½″-long pieces, then cut each piece lengthwise into strips, julienne style.
5. Cut onion into wedges ¼″ thick.
6. Peel carrot. Cut carrot and mushrooms into thin slices.
7. Combine thickener ingredients and mix well.
8. Heat wok and add 1 tbsp. oil. Add celery, onion, carrot, and mushrooms and stir-fry for 2 minutes over high heat, adding salt and sugar. Remove from wok and set aside.
9. Heat wok and add 2 tbsp. oil. Add chicken and stir-fry for 2 minutes over high heat.
10. Add chicken stock and bamboo shoots. Cover and cook for 3 minutes.
11. Add celery mixture. Mix thoroughly.
12. Stir in thickener. Cook for 30 seconds.
13. Remove from heat and mix in cashew nuts. Toss well and serve.

Advance preparation. Step 1 may be done 2 weeks in advance; store nuts in a covered container at room temperature. Steps 2–10 may be completed a few hours ahead and kept at room temperature.

CHICKEN IN HOT BEAN SAUCE
(Min See Gai)

1. Skin and bone chicken. Cut into ¾″ cubes. Place in a bowl.
2. Add seasoning ingredients to chicken. Mix well.
3. Cut green onions into ½″ pieces.
4. Peel carrot. Cut into ½″ dice.
5. Mash bean sauce to a paste.
6. Heat wok and add oil. Add garlic, chicken, and carrot and stir-fry for 2 minutes over high heat. Add hot bean sauce and mix thoroughly.
7. Add chicken stock. Bring mixture to a boil. Cover and cook for 2 minutes over high heat.
8. Add jicama and green onion. Cook for 1 minute.
9. Stir in thickener. Cook for 30 seconds. Serve.

Advance preparation: Steps 1–7 may be done a few hours in advance and kept at room temperature.

1 *whole chicken breast*
2 *green onions*
1 *medium-sized carrot*
1½ *tbsp. hot bean sauce*
2 *tbsp. oil*
1 *tbsp. finely chopped garlic*
½ *c. chicken stock*
¾ *c. diced (½″) jicama*

Seasoning:

½ *tsp. salt*
½ *tsp. sugar*
1 *tsp. thin soy sauce*
1 *tsp. oyster sauce*
1 *tsp. white wine*
1 *tsp. cornstarch*

Thickener:

2 *tsp. cornstarch, mixed well with 2 tsp. cold water*

Serves 4

CHICKEN WITH ASPARAGUS

(Lee Sun Gai Kau)

1 whole chicken breast, or 1 lb. chicken
   thighs
1½ lb. asparagus
1½ tbsp. salted black beans
1 tbsp. finely chopped garlic
1 tsp. crushed dried red chili pepper
   (optional)
3 tbsp. oil
¼ tsp. salt
½ tsp. sugar
¾ c. chicken stock

Seasoning:

1 tsp. salt
1 tsp. sugar
1 tsp. thin soy sauce
2 tsp. oyster sauce
1 tbsp. cornstarch

Thickener:

2 tsp. cornstarch, mixed well with 1½
   tbsp. cold water

Serves 6

1. Skin and bone chicken. Cut into pieces 1½″ by ½″. Place in a bowl.
2. Add seasoning ingredients to chicken. Mix well.
3. Break off and discard the tough base end of the asparagus. Cut each spear into 2″ lengths on the diagonal.
4. Rinse and drain black beans twice. Mash the beans with the butt end of a cleaver. Add garlic and chili pepper.
5. Heat wok and add 2 tbsp. oil. Add chicken and stir-fry for 3 minutes over high heat. Remove from wok and set aside.
6. Heat wok and add 1 tbsp. oil. Add black-bean mixture and cook for 30 seconds.
7. Add the asparagus and stir-fry for 2 minutes. Then add salt, sugar, chicken stock, and chicken. Bring to a boil. Cover and cook for 2 minutes over high heat.
8. Stir in thickener. Cook for 30 seconds. Serve.

Advance preparation: Steps 1–5 may be completed a few hours in advance and kept at room temperature.

CHICKEN WITH BEAN CAKE SAUCE
(Foo Yueh Gai)

1. Skin and bone chicken. Cut into pieces 1½" by ½".
2. Mash bean cake to a paste.
3. Cut green onions into ½" pieces.
4. Combine sauce ingredients and mix well.
5. Heat wok and add oil. Add garlic, green onions, chili pepper, and chicken and stir-fry for 2 minutes over high heat. Add bean cake and mix well.
6. Add sauce mixture. Bring quickly to a boil. Cover and cook for 5 minutes over high heat.
7. Stir in thickener. Cook for 30 seconds. Serve.

Advance preparation: The entire recipe may be prepared in advance and refrigerated. It will keep well for several days. Reheat on the stove or in a microwave oven.

Variation: Substitute 1 lb. lean pork butt, cut in julienne, for the chicken. The cooking time remains the same.

Note: Do not confuse fermented bean cake with fresh bean cake. See Ingredients Used in Chinese Cooking for additional information on this bottled product.

1½ lb. chicken breasts or thighs
2 tbsp. fermented bean cake
2 green onions
2 tbsp. oil
1 tbsp. finely chopped garlic
½ tsp. crushed dried red chili pepper (optional)

Sauce:

1 c. chicken stock
½ tsp. salt
1 tsp. sugar
1 tbsp. thin soy sauce
1 tbsp. white wine
1 tbsp. oyster sauce

Thickener:

1 tbsp. cornstarch, mixed well with 2 tbsp. cold water

Serves 4

CHICKEN WITH BROCCOLI
(Gai Chow Guy Lon)

1¼ lb. broccoli
1 whole chicken breast, or 1 lb. chicken
  thighs
2 tsp. slivered ginger root
1 green onion, slivered
3 tbsp. oil
½ tsp. salt
½ tsp. sugar
½ tsp. thin soy sauce
⅔ c. chicken stock

Seasoning:

½ tsp. salt
½ tsp. sugar
1 tsp. thin soy sauce
1 tsp. oyster sauce
1 tsp. white wine
dash of pepper
1 tbsp. cornstarch

Thickener:

2 tsp. cornstarch, mixed well with 2
  tsp. cold water

Serves 6

1. Peel off tough outer covering of broccoli stems. Cut stems and flowerets into thin slices on the diagonal.
2. Skin and bone chicken. Cut into pieces 1½" by ½". Place in a bowl.
3. Add seasoning ingredients, ginger, and green onion to chicken. Mix well.
4. Heat wok and add 1 tbsp. oil. Add broccoli and stir-fry for 2 minutes over high heat.
5. Add salt, sugar, soy sauce, and ⅓ c. chicken stock and bring to a boil. Cook, uncovered, for 2 minutes. Remove from wok and set aside.
6. Heat wok and add 2 tbsp. oil. Add chicken and stir-fry for 2 minutes over high heat.
7. Add ⅓ c. chicken stock. Cover and cook for 2 minutes over high heat.
8. Add broccoli. Mix thoroughly.
9. Stir in thickener. Cook for 30 seconds. Serve.

Advance preparation: Steps 1–7 may be completed several hours in advance and kept at room temperature.

Variation: Substitute 6 oz. fresh mushrooms, thinly sliced, and ½ lb. cabbage, sliced in pieces 2" wide, for the broccoli. The cooking time remains the same.

Serving suggestion: Serve with Winter Melon Soup, Sweet-and-Sour Pork, and Steamed Rice.

Note: When broccoli is cooked without a cover, it keeps its bright green color and stays nice and crunchy.

CHICKEN WITH CUCUMBER
(Wong Gua Gai)

1. Skin and bone chicken. Cut into pieces 1½″ by ½″. Place in a bowl.
2. Add seasoning ingredients to chicken. Mix well.
3. Peel cucumber so that you have narrow, alternating stripes of green and white. Cut cucumber in half lengthwise, then remove and discard seeds. Cut into thin slices on the diagonal.
4. Peel carrot. Cut into thin slices on the diagonal.
5. Combine sauce ingredients and mix well.
6. Heat wok and add oil. Add chicken and carrot and stir-fry for 2 minutes over high heat. Add chicken stock. Cover and cook for 2 minutes over high heat.
7. Add cucumber and green onions. Stir-fry for 1 minute. Stir in sauce mixture and mix well.
8. Stir in thickener. Cook for 30 seconds. Serve.

Advance preparation: Steps 1–5 may be completed several hours in advance and kept at room temperature.

1 whole chicken breast
1 small cucumber
1 carrot
2 tsp. finely chopped ginger root
3 tbsp. oil
½ c. chicken stock
2 green onions, slivered

Seasoning:

½ tsp. salt
½ tsp. sugar
1 tsp. thin soy sauce
2 tsp. oyster sauce
2 tsp. white wine
2 tsp. cornstarch

Sauce:

1½ tbsp. hot bean sauce
1 tbsp. catsup
1 tbsp. sesame oil
1 tbsp. oyster sauce
2 tsp. sugar

Thickener:

2 tsp. cornstarch, mixed well with 2 tsp. cold water

Serves 4

CUCUMBER AND CHICKEN SALAD
(Doong Wong Gua Gai)

1 English cucumber*
1 whole chicken breast
¼ tsp. salt
¼ head iceberg lettuce

Sauce:

½ tsp. dry mustard
1½ tbsp. Japanese rice vinegar
1 tbsp. sugar
1 tsp. thin soy sauce
½ tsp. chili paste with garlic
1 tbsp. oyster sauce
1 tbsp. sesame oil

*Regular cucumber may be substituted. After cutting lengthwise in step 1, scrape out seeds before slicing.

Serves 4

1. Cut cucumber in half lengthwise. Cut into very thin slices (less than ¼″) on the diagonal. You should have about 1½ c. Place in a bowl.
2. Place chicken breast on a plate. Sprinkle with salt and steam for 20 minutes. Remove from steamer, let cool, then remove and discard skin and bones. Shred meat by hand into ¼″ julienne, dropping it into the bowl with the cucumber as you work.
3. Combine sauce ingredients and mix well. Pour over chicken and cucumber and toss well. Refrigerate for 2 hours or more, but no more than 12 hours.
4. Just before serving, finely shred lettuce. You should have about 1 c. Add to chicken and cucumber and toss thoroughly. Remove to platter and serve.

Advance preparation: Steps 1–3 can be done 12 hours in advance and refrigerated.

Serving suggestion: This light, refreshing dish is ideal for hot-weather dining. It is also good to carry along to a potluck supper, as it can be served at room temperature rather than chilled.

CURRIED CHICKEN
(Gah-Li Gai)

1. Skin and bone chicken. Cut into pieces 1½" by ½".
2. Slice the mushrooms.
3. Cut yellow onion into wedges ¼" thick.
4. Combine sauce ingredients and mix well.
5. Heat wok and add oil. Add garlic, curry powder, and chicken and stir-fry for 2 minutes over high heat.
6. Mix in sauce mixture and bring to a boil. Cover and cook for 3 minutes over high heat.
7. Add yellow onion and mushrooms. Cover and cook for 2 minutes.
8. Stir in thickener ingredients and green onion. Cook for 30 seconds. Serve.

Advance preparation: The entire recipe may be prepared a few days in advance and refrigerated.

1 whole chicken breast
¼ lb. fresh mushrooms
½ medium-sized yellow onion
2 tbsp. oil
1 tbsp. finely chopped garlic
1 tbsp. curry powder
1 green onion, finely chopped

Sauce:

1 tsp. salt
1 tsp. sugar
1 tbsp. white wine
1 tbsp. oyster sauce
1 c. chicken stock

Thickener:

1 tbsp. cornstarch, mixed well with 2 tbsp. cold water
1½ tsp. sesame oil

Serves 4

GARLIC CHICKEN
(Hsuen Gee Gai)

1½ lb. chicken thighs
20 snow peas
1 medium-sized yellow onion
2 tbsp. oil
1 tbsp. finely chopped garlic
2 tsp. finely chopped ginger root
½ c. chicken stock
3 green onions, slivered

Seasoning:

1 tsp. salt
1 tsp. sugar
2 tsp. thin soy sauce
1 tbsp. oyster sauce
1 tbsp. white wine
1 tbsp. cornstarch

Sauce:

1 tbsp. hoisin sauce
1 tbsp. catsup
1½ tsp. dark soy sauce
1 tsp. crushed dried red chili pepper
1 tbsp. sesame oil

Serves 4

1. Skin and bone chicken. Cut into pieces 1½″ by ½″. Place in a bowl.
2. Add seasoning ingredients to chicken. Mix well.
3. Remove tips from snow peas. Cut into 1″ pieces on the diagonal.
4. Cut yellow onion into wedges ¼″ thick.
5. Combine sauce ingredients and mix well.
6. Heat wok and add oil. Add garlic, ginger, and chicken and stir-fry for 3 minutes over high heat. Add snow peas, yellow onion, and chicken stock. Cover and cook for 2 minutes over high heat.
7. Add sauce mixture and green onions. Mix thoroughly and serve.

Advance preparation: Steps 1–6 may be done a few hours in advance and kept at room temperature. Reheat for 30 seconds before completing recipe.

Variation: Substitute ¼ lb. fresh mushrooms, sliced, and ¼ lb. summer squash, thinly sliced, for the snow peas and yellow onion. Add in step 6. The cooking time remains the same.

Hunan Chicken
(Hunan Gai)

1. Boil dried mushrooms in water to cover for 10 minutes. Rinse, drain, and squeeze dry. Cut off and discard stems. Cut mushrooms into strips, julienne style.
2. Bring 1 c. chicken stock to a boil. Add mushrooms. Bring quickly to a boil, cover, and cook over medium heat for 10 minutes. Stir occasionally and be sure liquid does not cook away. (If it does, add more chicken stock.) Remove from heat, drain mushrooms, and set aside.
3. Skin and bone chicken. Cut into pieces 1½" by ½". Place in a bowl.
4. Add seasoning ingredients to chicken. Mix well.
5. Remove tips from snow peas. Cut peas into ½" pieces on the diagonal.
6. If using fresh water chestnuts, peel and remove and discard top and root ends. Cut fresh or canned water chestnuts into thin slices.
7. To make the sauce, mash bean sauce to a paste. Add remaining ingredients and mix well.
8. Heat wok and add oil. Add garlic and chicken and stir-fry for 2 minutes over high heat. Add ⅓ c. chicken stock, cover, and cook for 2 minutes over high heat.
9. Add mushrooms, snow peas, water chestnuts or jicama, green onions, and sauce mixture. Stir-fry for 1 minute over high heat.
10. Stir in thickener. Cook for 30 seconds. Serve.

Advance preparation: Steps 1–8 may be completed a few hours in advance and kept at room temperature.

Variation: Substitute ¼ lb. fresh mushrooms, sliced, for Chinese dried mushrooms. Omit steps 1 and 2 and 1 c. of the chicken stock. Add fresh mushrooms in step 9.

10 small Chinese dried black
   mushrooms
1⅓ c. chicken stock
1 whole chicken breast
10 snow peas
5 fresh or canned water chestnuts, or
   ½ c. shredded jicama
2 tbsp. oil
1 tbsp. finely chopped garlic
2 green onions, slivered

Seasoning:

¼ tsp. salt
¼ tsp. sugar
1 tsp. thin soy sauce
2 tsp. cornstarch

Sauce:

1 tbsp. hot bean sauce
1 tbsp. oyster sauce
1 tsp. dark soy sauce
2 tsp. sesame oil
2 tsp. sugar

Thickener:

2 tsp. cornstarch, mixed well with 2
   tsp. cold water

Serves 4

JENNIE'S PAN-FRIED CHICKEN
(Jin Gai)

1 whole chicken breast
1/2 c. cornstarch
1/4 c. oil for pan-frying
2 tbsp. oil for stir-frying
1 tsp. finely chopped ginger root
2 tsp. finely chopped garlic
1 green onion, finely chopped

Seasoning:

1/4 tsp. salt
1/4 tsp. sugar
1 tsp. thin soy sauce

Sauce:

3 tbsp. oyster sauce
2 tbsp. white wine
1 1/2 tbsp. sugar
1 tbsp. sesame oil
1/4 tsp. crushed dried red chili pepper
   (optional)

Serves 4

1. Skin and bone chicken. Cut into pieces 1½" by ½". Place in a bowl.
2. Add seasoning ingredients to chicken. Mix well.
3. Combine sauce ingredients and mix well.
4. Coat chicken pieces with cornstarch immediately before frying.
5. Heat frying pan, preferably one with a nonstick coating. Add ¼ c. oil and heat for 30 seconds. Add chicken pieces. Fry in hot oil for 5 minutes. Remove and drain on paper towels.
6. Heat wok and add 2 tbsp. oil. Add ginger, garlic, and green onion and stir-fry for 30 seconds over high heat.
7. Add sauce mixture and chicken pieces. Mix well and serve.

Advance preparation: You may pan-fry the chicken pieces several hours in advance. Keep at room temperature.

Note: This is one recipe you will have to make yourself. You will not find it on any restaurant menu.

LEMON CHICKEN
(Ling Mont Gai)

1. To prepare the batter, lightly beat egg white with a fork. Add cornstarch, baking soda, baking powder, and water. Mix thoroughly. Set aside at room temperature for at least 5 hours, or as long as overnight. If prepared more than a day in advance, refrigerate.
2. Skin and bone chicken breast. Cut into pieces 1½" by ½". Leave drumettes whole. Place chicken in a bowl.
3. Add seasoning ingredients to chicken. Mix well.
4. Cut lemon into thin slices. Cut each slice in half to make about 10 half slices.
5. Combine sauce ingredients in a small pan. Add lemon slices and bring to a boil. Stir in thickener. Cook for 30 seconds. Set aside.
6. Heat oil in wok to 325 degrees. Add chicken pieces to batter and coat thoroughly. Drop chicken, a piece at a time, into hot oil, stirring after each addition to keep chicken from sticking to pan bottom. Deep-fry for 3 minutes. Remove chicken and drain on paper towels. Arrange on a serving platter.
7. Meanwhile, reheat sauce (including lemon slices) to a boil. Pour over hot chicken and serve.

Advance preparation: Step 1 may be done 2 days in advance and refrigerated. Steps 2–4 may be completed the day before and refrigerated.

*You may be surprised to see that I have used this commercial product here, but I have found that the easiest way to assure the success of this recipe is to use lemon juice from the familiar "plastic lemon" (this juice is also available in bottles). This is because the juice from fresh lemons is often too sour and adversely affects the taste of the dish. If you want to serve the same dish I serve, then use ReaLemon.

1 whole chicken breast, or 10
   drumettes
½ medium-sized lemon
3 c. oil for deep-frying

Batter:

egg white from 1 large egg
2½ tbsp. cornstarch
¼ tsp. baking soda
½ tsp. baking powder
1 tbsp. cold water

Seasoning:

⅓ tsp. salt
⅓ tsp. sugar
¾ tsp. thin soy sauce
1 tsp. oyster sauce
2 tsp. white wine

Sauce:

⅓ c. cold water
3 tbsp. ReaLemon brand lemon juice*
1 tsp. thin soy sauce
¼ c. sugar
1 tsp. catsup
1 tsp. sesame oil

Thickener:

1¾ tsp. cornstarch, mixed well with 2
   tsp. cold water.

Serves 4

Mo Shu Chicken with Mandarin Pancakes
(Muk Shui Gai Bok Bengh)

Mandarin Pancakes
(Bok Bengh)

2 c. all-purpose flour
⅔ c. water, boiling
3 tbsp. cold water
sesame oil
about 2 tbsp. oil

Makes 8

1. Place flour in a mixing bowl. Gradually add boiling water while stirring with chopsticks. Add cold water and mix well.
2. Using your hands, shape dough into a ball. On a lightly floured board, knead until smooth (about 30 seconds). It should have the texture of chocolate-chip cookie dough. Cover dough with cloth and let rest for 15 minutes.
3. Lightly flour board and turn dough out onto it. Knead for 30 seconds. With the palms of your hands, roll dough back and forth on the board until it forms a rope about 12″ long. Cut the rope into 8 equal pieces.
4. Flatten each piece on the board with your palm, then roll out into a circle 8″ in diameter. Roll out a second circle in the same way.
5. Lightly brush top surface of 1 pancake with sesame oil and place second pancake on top. (Pancakes are cooked in pairs to obtain a soft rather than a crispy texture. Sesame oil aids in separating pancakes after cooking.) Repeat with remaining dough. Stack pairs, placing waxed paper between each pair of pancakes to prevent sticking.
6. Heat a nonstick or cast-iron skillet over medium heat. Add ½ tbsp. oil. (Be sure to heat skillet sufficiently or the pancakes will stick.) Add a pair of pancakes, cover skillet, and cook for 1½ minutes. Top pancake should bubble slightly and bottom pancake will have light golden-brown spots. Flip pancake, cover, and cook until golden brown on the second side (about 45 seconds). Remove from skillet.
7. Separate pancakes by pulling them apart gently. Restack in a pie plate and cover with foil. Place in an oven preheated to 350 degrees. Immediately turn off oven heat. Cook the remaining pairs of pancakes, separate, and add to the pie plate. Once the pancakes have been separated, they may be stacked without fear of them sticking together.

Advance preparation: Cooked pancakes will keep for several days in the refrigerator. Reheat by steaming for 2 minutes. They may also be frozen for up to 3 months. Reheat by steaming without thawing for 3 minutes.

Serving suggestion: Mo shu chicken, or the beef or prawn variation, may be served as a first course or with other dishes for a main course. You may also omit the pancakes and serve romaine lettuce to use as wrappers.

MO SHU CHICKEN FILLING
(Muk Shui Gai)

1. Soak fungus for 15 minutes in warm water to cover. Drain, rinse thoroughly, and drain again. Remove and discard stems. Cut fungus into 1″ slivers; you should have about 1 c. Alternatively, slice the fresh mushrooms.
2. Skin and bone chicken. Cut chicken meat into thin strips, julienne style. Place in a bowl.
3. Add seasoning ingredients to chicken. Mix well.
4. Remove tips from snow peas. Cut into julienne strips. Alternatively, cut cabbage into julienne strips.
5. Mash bean sauce to a paste.
6. Heat wok and add 1 tbsp. oil. Add eggs and scramble over medium-high heat until just set. Remove from wok and set aside.
7. Heat wok and add 1 tbsp. oil. Add fungus or mushrooms and snow peas or cabbage and stir-fry for 1 minute over medium heat, adding salt and sugar. Remove from wok and set aside.
8. Heat wok and add 2½ tbsp. oil. Add chicken and stir-fry for 2 minutes over high heat.
9. Add bean sauce and mix well. Add chicken stock, cover, and cook over high heat for 2 minutes.
10. Stir in thickener ingredients. Cook for 30 seconds.
11. Add reserved vegetables and cooked eggs. Mix well. Transfer to a serving platter.
12. Each person "rolls his own" pancake and eats it like a burrito. Spread about 1 tsp. hoisin sauce on the center of the pancake (fig. 1). Add 3 tbsp. meat mixture and a few slivers of green onion. Fold the left side toward the center about 1″ from the edge (fig. 2). This fold keeps the juices from dripping out. Then roll up from the bottom to the top (fig. 3). When all the pancakes have been eaten, pass lettuce leaves for guests to use as wrappers for remaining mo shu mixture.

Advance preparation: Steps 1–8 may be done a few hours in advance and kept at room temperature.

Mo Shu Beef or Mo Shu Shrimp Variation: Substitute 1 lb. flank steak or 1 lb. medium-sized prawns in the shell. If using flank steak, cut lengthwise (with the grain of the meat) into 3 equal strips each about 1½″ wide. Cut each strip across the grain into thin slices. If using prawns, shell, devein, wash, and drain prawns. Cut lengthwise into strips. Use the same seasoning as in mo shu chicken for both variations. Follow steps 1–7. Then heat wok and add 2½ tbsp. oil. Add beef or prawns and stir-fry for 2 minutes over high heat. Add bean sauce and mix well. Add ¼ c. chicken stock (note the reduced amount of chicken stock). Bring to a boil uncovered. Now proceed as directed in steps 10–12.

4 pieces dried black fungus, or 6 oz. fresh mushrooms
1 whole chicken breast
30 snow peas, or ¼ lb. cabbage
2 tsp. bean sauce*
4½ tbsp. oil
3 eggs, lightly beaten
dash of salt
dash of sugar
⅓ c. chicken stock
romaine lettuce leaves

Seasoning:

¼ tsp. salt
½ tsp. sugar
1 tsp. thin soy sauce
1 tbsp. oyster sauce
1 tbsp. white wine
1 tbsp. cornstarch

Thickener:

1 tbsp. cornstarch, mixed well with 1 tbsp. cold water
1 tbsp. sesame oil

Condiments:

about ¼ c. hoisin sauce
3 green onions (white part only), slivered

*Use regular bean sauce, not hot bean sauce.

Serves 4

PINEAPPLE CHICKEN
(Bwo Luo Gai)

1 whole chicken breast
2 c. oil for deep-frying

Batter:

egg white from 1 large egg
2½ tbsp. cornstarch
¼ tsp. baking soda
½ tsp. baking powder
1 tbsp. cold water

Seasoning:

½ tsp. salt
½ tsp. sugar
1 tsp. thin soy sauce
1 tsp. oyster sauce
dash of pepper

Sauce:

1 stalk celery
¼ c. water
½ tbsp. catsup
1 tbsp. distilled white vinegar
1 can (8 oz.) chunk-style pineapple
   with juice

Thickener:

1 tbsp. cornstarch, mixed well with 1
   tbsp. cold water

Serves 4

1. To prepare the batter, lightly beat egg white with a fork. Add cornstarch, baking soda, baking powder, and water. Mix thoroughly. Let stand for at least 5 hours, or as long as overnight at room temperature. If prepared more than a day in advance, refrigerate.
2. Skin and bone chicken. Cut into pieces 1½″ by ½″. Place in a bowl.
3. Add seasoning ingredients to chicken. Mix well.
4. Make the sauce. Peel celery. Cut into 1½″-long pieces. Cut each piece lengthwise in strips, julienne style.
5. In a saucepan or wok, combine all sauce ingredients and bring quickly to a boil.
6. Stir in thickener. Cook for 30 seconds. Remove from heat.
7. Heat oil in wok to 325 degrees. Add chicken pieces to batter and coat thoroughly. Drop chicken, a piece at a time, into hot oil, stirring after each addition to make sure chicken doesn't stick to pan bottom. Deep-fry for 3 minutes. Remove chicken and drain on paper towels. Arrange on a serving platter.
8. Meanwhile, reheat pineapple sauce to a boil. Pour over hot chicken and serve immediately.

Advance preparation: The batter may be prepared 2 days in advance and refrigerated. Steps 2–6 may be completed a few hours in advance and kept at room temperature.

PINE NUT CHICKEN

(Tsung Mai Gai)

1. Skin and bone chicken. Cut into pieces 1½" by ½". Place in a bowl.
2. Add marinade ingredients to chicken and mix well. Marinate for 1 hour at room temperature, or overnight in the refrigerator.
3. Toast pine nuts in a 325-degree oven until golden brown (about 5 minutes).
4. Peel celery. Cut into 1½"-long pieces. Cut each piece lengthwise into strips, julienne style.
5. Cut onion into wedges ¼" thick.
6. Combine sauce ingredients and mix well.
7. Heat wok and add oil. Add garlic and chicken pieces and stir-fry over high heat for 2 minutes.
8. Add chicken stock, onion, and celery. Cover and cook for 2 minutes.
9. Add sauce. Cook for 30 seconds.
10. Stir in thickener. Cook for 30 seconds.
11. Remove from heat and toss in toasted pine nuts. Serve.

Advance preparation: You may toast pine nuts (step 3) up to 2 weeks in advance and store them in a closed container at room temperature. Steps 1 and 2 and 4–8 may be completed a few hours in advance. Reheat before proceeding to step 9.

Variation: Snow peas or jicama may be substituted for the celery and red onion. Remove tips from 30 snow peas and cut peas into ½" pieces on the diagonal. Prepare ¾ c. shredded jicama. Add snow peas or jicama in step 8; cooking time remains the same.

1 whole chicken breast
⅓ c. pine nuts
1 stalk celery
½ small red onion
2½ tbsp. oil
1 tbsp. finely chopped garlic
⅓ c. chicken stock

Marinade:

½ tsp. salt
½ tsp. sugar
1 tsp. thin soy sauce
2 tsp. oyster sauce
1 tbsp. white wine
2 tbsp. cornstarch

Sauce:

1 tbsp. oyster sauce
1 tbsp. sesame oil
1 tbsp. hoisin sauce

Thickener:

2 tsp. cornstarch, mixed well with 2 tsp. cold water

Serves 4

SESAME CHICKEN
(Gee Mah Gai)

2 tbsp. raw white sesame seeds
1 whole chicken breast, or 10
   drumettes
2 c. oil for deep-frying
1 tbsp. oil for stir-frying
1 tbsp. finely chopped garlic

Batter:

egg white from 1 large egg
2½ tbsp. cornstarch
¼ tsp. baking soda
½ tsp. baking powder
1 tbsp. cold water

Seasoning:

⅓ tsp. salt
⅓ tsp. sugar
2 tsp. oyster sauce

Sauce:

¼ c. chicken stock
1½ tbsp. thin soy sauce
2 tbsp. sesame oil
2 tbsp. sugar
2 tbsp. white wine
1 tbsp. oyster sauce
½ tsp. dried crushed red chili pepper
   (optional)

Thickener:

2 tsp. cornstarch, mixed well with 2
   tsp. cold water

Serves 4

1. To prepare the batter, lightly beat egg white with a fork. Add cornstarch, baking soda, baking powder, and water. Mix thoroughly. Let stand for at least 5 hours, or as long as overnight at room temperature. If prepared more than a day in advance, refrigerate.
2. Toast sesame seeds in a dry (no oil) frying pan over medium heat until golden brown (about 1 minute).
3. Skin and bone chicken breast. Cut into pieces 1½″ by ½″. Leave drumettes whole. Place chicken in a bowl.
4. Add seasoning ingredients to chicken. Mix well.
5. Combine sauce ingredients and mix well.
6. Heat 2 c. oil in wok to 325 degrees. Add chicken pieces to batter and coat thoroughly. Drop chicken, a piece at a time, into hot oil, stirring after each addition to make sure chicken doesn't stick to pan bottom. Deep-fry for 4 minutes. Remove chicken and drain on paper towels. Remove oil from wok.
7. Heat wok and add 1 tbsp. oil. Add garlic and stir-fry for 20–30 seconds. Add sauce mixture and bring quickly to a boil.
8. Stir in thickener. Cook for 30 seconds.
9. Add chicken to wok and mix well. Remove to platter. Sprinkle with sesame seeds and serve.

Advance preparation: The sesame seeds may be toasted 2 weeks in advance and stored in a closed container at room temperature. The batter may be made up to 2 days in advance and refrigerated. The chicken may be deep-fried a few hours in advance and kept at room temperature. It does not need to be reheated before adding to the wok in step 9. The hot sauce will heat the chicken sufficiently.

SOY SAUCE CHICKEN WINGS

(See Yau Gai Yick)

1. In a 2-quart saucepan, bring water to a boil. Add star anise and ginger and boil, uncovered, for 10 minutes. There should be at least 1 c. of liquid remaining; if not, add water to make 1 c.
2. Combine sauce ingredients and add to saucepan. Stir well and bring to a boil.
3. Add chicken wings. Lower the heat, cover, and simmer for 15 minutes. Turn off heat and let stand for 30 minutes.
4. Remove chicken wings from sauce and serve hot or at room temperature. Reserve the sauce for future use, storing in a tightly covered container in the refrigerator. (See variations, below, for additional uses for sauce.)

Advance preparation: The entire recipe may be completed a few hours in advance and kept at room temperature. Simply reheat in the sauce if you wish to serve the wings hot.

Variations:
   Have the butcher cut a slab of spareribs (1½ to 2 lb.) lengthwise into strips 1½" wide. Cut ribs apart. Simmer spareribs in prepared sauce for 30 minutes. Turn off heat and let stand for 30 minutes. Remove from sauce and serve hot or at room temperature.
   Simmer 2 squabs (about 1 lb. each) in prepared sauce for 30 minutes. Turn off heat and let stand for 30 minutes. Remove from sauce. To serve squabs, remove thighs and drumsticks and cut each into 2 pieces. Leave wings whole. Cut breasts and backs into 2" by 1½" pieces. Serve hot or at room temperature.

1½ c. water
3 whole star anise
1 slice ginger root (about ¾" thick and 1" in diameter), peeled and crushed
2 lb. chicken wings

Sauce:

1 c. dark soy sauce
1 tbsp. white wine
1 c. firmly packed brown sugar

Serves 4

CANTONESE STEAMED CHICKEN
(Jing Gai)

10 small Chinese dried black
    mushrooms
4 dried red dates (optional)
14 dried lily flowers
2 pieces dried black fungus
2 lb. chicken parts
1 tbsp. slivered ginger root
2 green onions, slivered

Seasoning:

1¼ tsp. salt
1 tsp. sugar
1 tsp. thin soy sauce
1 tsp. dark soy sauce
2 tsp. oyster sauce
1 tbsp. white wine
dash of pepper
1¾ tbsp. cornstarch
1 tsp. cold water

Serves 6

1. Soak mushrooms, dried red dates, lily flowers, and black fungus for 15 minutes in warm water to cover. Drain, rinse well, and squeeze dry.
2. Skin and bone chicken. Cut into pieces 1½" by ½". Place chicken in a shallow dish.
3. Add seasoning ingredients to chicken. Mix well.
4. Remove and discard stems of mushrooms. Cut into thin strips, julienne style.
5. Remove and discard date seeds. Cut into thin strips, julienne style.
6. Cut off and discard ½" from the pointed end of each lily flower. Cut each needle in half crosswise.
7. Remove and discard stems from black fungus. Cut into 1" slivers. You should have about ⅓ c.
8. Add mushrooms, red dates, black fungus, lily flowers, ginger, and green onion to chicken. Mix thoroughly.
9. Steam for 20 minutes.

Advance preparation: Steps 1–8 may be completed several hours in advance and kept at room temperature.

SZECHUAN SPICED CHICKEN
(See Chuen Gai)

1. Skin and bone chicken. Cut into pieces 1½" by ½". Place in a bowl.
2. Add seasoning ingredients to chicken. Mix well.
3. If using broccoli, peel off tough outer skin of stalk with a small knife. Cut stalk in half lengthwise, then cut into thin slices on the diagonal. You should have about ¾ c. If using snow peas, remove tips. Cut into ½" pieces on the diagonal.
4. Combine sauce ingredients and mix well.
5. Heat wok and add ½ tbsp. oil. Add broccoli or snow peas and stir-fry for 1 minute over high heat, adding salt and sugar. Remove from wok and set aside.
6. Heat wok and add 1½ tbsp. oil. Add chicken and stir-fry for 2 minutes over high heat.
7. Add chicken stock and bring quickly to a boil. Cover and cook for 2 minutes over high heat.
8. Add sauce mixture and stir well.
9. Add broccoli or snow peas and green onions. Mix well.
10. Stir in thickener. Cook for 30 seconds. Serve.

1 whole chicken breast
1 stalk broccoli (without flowerets), or
   25 snow peas
2 tbsp. oil
¼ tsp. salt
¼ tsp. sugar
½ c. chicken stock
2 green onions, slivered

Sauce:

1 tsp. chili paste with garlic*
1½ tsp. hoisin sauce
1 tsp. sugar
2½ tsp. Japanese rice vinegar
1 tsp. dark soy sauce
1 tsp. oyster sauce
2 tsp. sesame oil

Seasoning:

⅓ tsp. salt
½ tsp. sugar
½ tsp. thin soy sauce
1 tsp. oyster sauce
2 tsp. white wine
2 tsp. cornstarch

Thickener:

2 tsp. cornstarch, mixed well with 1
   tbsp. cold water

*Chili paste with garlic is quite spicy. If you prefer a milder dish, reduce amount to ½ tsp.

Serves 4

DUCK AND POTATOES
(Sheu-Jai Mun Op)

4–5 lb. duck
6 medium-sized red potatoes
20 small Chinese dried black
 mushrooms
2 green onions
2 tbsp. oil
3 c. chicken stock, or as needed
1 tbsp. finely chopped garlic

Sauce:

1 tbsp. bean sauce
2 tbsp. preserved red bean curd
1½ tsp. salt
½ tsp. five-spice powder
1 tbsp. sugar
1 tbsp. white wine
2 tbsp. thin soy sauce
2 tbsp. oyster sauce
5 whole star anise
dash of pepper

Thickener:

2 tbsp. cornstarch, mixed well with 2
 tbsp. cold water

Serves 8

1. With a cleaver, chop duck in half, then in quarters. Cut each quarter into pieces approximately 2" wide.
2. Peel potatoes. Cut into 1½" cubes. Immerse in cold water.
3. Boil dried mushrooms in water to cover for 10 minutes. Drain, rinse, and squeeze dry. Remove and discard stems.
4. Cut green onions into 1" pieces.
5. Heat wok and add oil. Add duck pieces and stir-fry until pieces are nicely browned (about 5 minutes). Remove duck from wok, draining off any excess oil.
6. Prepare the sauce. Mash bean sauce and red bean curd to a paste. Add remaining ingredients and mix well.
7. In a wok or large stew pot, bring 3 c. chicken stock to a boil. Add duck, mushrooms, green onions, garlic, and sauce mixture. Bring quickly to a boil, cover, reduce heat to medium, and cook for 35 minutes.
8. Drain potatoes, add to wok, cover, and cook for 15 minutes more. There should be at least 1½ c. of liquid remaining. If not, add sufficient chicken stock to make 1½ c.
9. Stir in thickener. Cook for 1 minute. (You may find you need more thickener for the sauce to achieve a good consistency. Just mix up another batch and stir it in.) Serve.

Advance preparation: Steps 1–8 may be completed several hours in advance and kept at room temperature. This dish keeps well! You will find it tastes just as good the next day.

Variations:

Use a whole chicken (about 3½ lb.), quartered, in place of the duck. Reduce the chicken stock to 2 c. and reduce the cooking time in step 7 to 20 minutes.

Substitute 3 lb. beef stew meat, cut into 1½" cubes, for the duck. Use the same cooking time as for the duck.

MEAT

BEEF IN OYSTER SAUCE

(Ho Yau Ngow Yuk)

1 lb. flank steak
2 tbsp. oil
1 tbsp. finely chopped garlic
3 green onions, slivered
½ c. chicken stock
2 tbsp. oyster sauce

Marinade:

1 tsp. salt
½ tsp. sugar
1 tsp. thin soy sauce
2 tsp. white wine
dash of pepper
1 tbsp. cornstarch
1 tbsp. slivered ginger root

Serves 4

1. Cut flank steak lengthwise (with grain of meat) into 3 equal strips each approximately 1½″ wide. Cut each strip across the grain into thin slices. Place in a bowl.
2. Add marinade ingredients to beef. Mix well and marinate for 1 hour at room temperature.
3. Heat wok and add oil. Add chopped garlic and stir-fry for 30 seconds over high heat.
4. Add beef and stir-fry for 3 minutes over high heat.
5. Add green onions, chicken stock, and oyster sauce. Bring to a boil and serve.

Advance preparation: Steps 1–4 may be completed a few hours in advance and kept at room temperature.

Serving suggestion: This dish can be served as one element of a multicourse meal or it can be spooned over rice and garnished with a fried egg, sunny-side up, for a one-plate dinner. It is also good atop noodles for a hearty lunch.

CANTONESE BEEF STEW
(Ngow Nom)

1. Trim fat from beef. Cut beef into 1½" cubes.
2. Combine bean sauce and red bean curd and mash to a paste. Add five-spice powder, star anise, green onions, salt, sugar, thin soy sauce, and white wine.
3. Heat wok and add oil. Add garlic, ginger, and beef and stir-fry for 4 minutes over high heat.
4. Transfer meat to a large pot. Add sauce mixture from step 2 and 3 c. chicken stock. Bring quickly to a boil, reduce heat to medium, cover, and cook 1 hour. Stir occasionally. There should be at least 1½ c. of liquid remaining. If not, add chicken stock to make 1½ c.
5. Combine thickener ingredients and stir in. Cook for 1 minute. Serve.

Advance preparation: The entire recipe may be completed a few days in advance and refrigerated. The stew tastes even better reheated.

3½ lb. beef stew meat
1 tbsp. bean sauce
1 tbsp. preserved red bean curd
¼ tsp. five-spice powder
3 whole star anise
2 whole green onions
1 tsp. salt
1½ tsp. sugar
1 tbsp. thin soy sauce
1 tbsp. white wine
2 tbsp. oil
2 garlic cloves, crushed
1 slice ginger root (about 1" thick and 1" in diameter), peeled and crushed
3 c. chicken stock, or as needed

Thickener:

2 tbsp. cornstarch, mixed well with 2 tbsp. cold water
2 tbsp. oyster sauce

Serves 8

BEEF WITH ASPARAGUS

(Ngow Yuk Lee Sum)

1 lb. flank steak
1½ lb. asparagus
2½ tbsp. salted black beans
1 tbsp. finely chopped garlic
1 tsp. crushed dried red chili pepper
  (optional)
3½ tbsp. oil
½ tsp. salt
½ tsp. sugar
¾ c. chicken stock

Seasoning:

1 tsp. salt
1 tsp. sugar
1 tbsp. white wine
1 tsp. thin soy sauce
1 tbsp. oyster sauce
1 tbsp. cornstarch

Thickener:

1½ tbsp. cornstarch, mixed well with 3
  tbsp. cold water
1 tbsp. sesame oil

Serves 6

1. Cut flank steak lengthwise (with grain of meat) into 3 equal strips each approximately 1½" wide. Cut each strip across the grain into thin slices. Place in a bowl.
2. Add seasoning ingredients to beef and mix well.
3. Break off and discard tough base end of asparagus. Cut each spear into ½" slices on the diagonal.
4. Rinse and drain black beans twice. Mash to a paste with the butt end of a cleaver. Add garlic and chili pepper.
5. Heat wok and add 2 tbsp. oil. Add beef and stir-fry for 2 minutes over high heat. Remove from wok and set aside.
6. Heat wok and add 1½ tbsp. oil. Add black-bean mixture and stir-fry for 30 seconds over high heat.
7. Add asparagus and stir-fry for 2 minutes over high heat. Add salt, sugar, and chicken stock. Bring quickly to a boil and cook, uncovered, for 2 minutes.
8. Add cooked beef and mix well.
9. Stir in thickener ingredients. Cook for 30 seconds. Serve.

Advance preparation: Steps 1–5 may be done a few hours in advance and kept at room temperature.

Variations: Substitute 1 lb. broccoli or 1 lb. bok choy for the asparagus. Cut according to directions in Cutting Techniques section. Cook in the same manner as asparagus.

HUNAN BEEF
(Hunan Ngow Yuk)

1. Cut flank steak lengthwise (with grain of meat) into 3 equal strips each approximately 1½" wide. Cut each strip across the grain into thin slices. Place in a bowl.
2. To make the marinade, mix baking soda with warm water and add to the meat. (The baking soda helps to tenderize the meat.) Add the remaining marinade ingredients and mix well. Marinate for at least 5 hours, or as long as overnight in the refrigerator.
3. Heat wok and add oil. Add garlic and ginger and stir-fry for 30 seconds over high heat.
4. Add beef and stir-fry for 3 minutes over high heat.
5. Add green onions, hoisin sauce, and chili paste. Stir well and serve.

Advance preparation: Steps 1 and 2 may be completed a day in advance and refrigerated.

1 lb. flank steak
2½ tbsp. oil
1 tbsp. finely chopped garlic
1 tbsp. finely chopped ginger root
2 green onions, slivered
1 tbsp. hoisin sauce
½ tsp. chili paste with garlic

Marinade:

½ tsp. baking soda
1 tsp. warm water
½ tsp. salt
½ tsp. sugar
2 tsp. dark soy sauce
1 tsp. thin soy sauce
1 tbsp. oyster sauce
1½ tbsp. cornstarch
1 tbsp. sesame oil
1½ tbsp. white wine
egg white from 1 large egg

Serves 6

MONGOLIAN BEEF
(Hoisin Jerng Ngow Yuk)

1 lb. flank steak
2 tbsp. oil
2 tbsp. finely chopped garlic
2 green onions, slivered

Seasoning:

1 tsp. salt
2 tsp. sugar
2 tsp. thin soy sauce
1 tbsp. oyster sauce
dash of pepper
1 tbsp. white wine
1½ tbsp. cornstarch

Sauce:

¼ c. chicken stock
2 tbsp. hoisin sauce
2 tsp. catsup
½ tsp. crushed dried red chili pepper
  (optional)

Serves 4

1. Cut flank steak lengthwise (with grain of meat) into 3 equal strips each approximately 1½″ wide. Cut each strip across the grain into thin slices. Place in a bowl.
2. Add seasoning ingredients to beef. Mix well.
3. Combine sauce ingredients and mix well.
4. Heat wok and add oil. Add garlic and stir-fry for 30 seconds over high heat.
5. Add beef and green onions and stir-fry for 3 minutes over high heat.
6. Add sauce mixture. Mix thoroughly and cook for 1 minute. Serve.

Advance preparation: Steps 1–5 may be completed a few hours in advance and kept at room temperature.

Serving suggestion: Serve with Steamed Rice or Noodles in Oyster Sauce and Bean Sprouts with Mixed Vegetables.

TOMATO BEEF
(Fon Kehr Ngow Yuk)

1. Cut flank steak lengthwise (with grain of meat) into 3 equal strips, each approximately 1½″ wide. Cut each strip across the grain into thin slices. Place in a bowl.
2. Add seasoning ingredients to beef. Mix well.
3. Peel celery. Cut into 1½″-long pieces. Cut each piece lengthwise into strips, julienne style.
4. Cut bell peppers in half. Remove and discard seeds. Cut into pieces 1″ by ½″.
5. Cut tomatoes in half. Cut each half into 5 equal wedges.
6. Heat wok and add 1 tbsp. oil. Add celery and bell pepper and stir-fry for 2 minutes over high heat. Remove from wok and set aside.
7. Heat wok and add 2 tbsp. oil. Add beef and stir-fry for 3 minutes. Remove from wok and set aside with vegetables.
8. Put tomatoes in wok. Combine vinegar, sugar, salt, and catsup, and add to pan. Bring quickly to a boil.
9. Add vegetables and beef. Return to a boil.
10. Stir in thickener ingredients. Cook for 1 minute. Serve.

Advance preparation: Steps 1–8 may be done a few hours in advance and kept at room temperature.

1 lb. flank steak
3 stalks celery
2 bell peppers
4 tomatoes
3 tbsp. oil
2 tsp. cider vinegar
2 tbsp. sugar
½ tsp. salt
2 tbsp. catsup

Seasoning:

1 tsp. salt
½ tsp. sugar
1 tsp. thin soy sauce
1 tsp. oyster sauce
dash of pepper
1 tbsp. cornstarch
1 green onion, slivered

Thickener:

1 tbsp. cornstarch, mixed well with 2
   tbsp. cold water
2 tsp. dark soy sauce

Serves 6

CHINESE BARBECUED PORK
(Cha Siu)

1 lb. lean pork butt
2 c. water

Marinade:

¼ tsp. salt
dash of pepper
1¼ tbsp. sugar
2 tsp. thin soy sauce
½ tsp. roasting salt
1½ tsp. oyster sauce
1½ tsp. hoisin sauce
2 tsp. white wine
1 tbsp. honey

Serves 5

1. Cut meat into strips approximately 2″ wide and no more than 1″ thick.
2. Combine marinade ingredients in a large bowl. Add meat and marinate for at least 5 hours in the refrigerator.
3. Preheat oven to 375 degrees.
4. Pour water into a roasting pan. Put rack in pan and arrange pork on rack. Pour marinade over pork. Roast, uncovered, for 30 minutes, basting twice with pan juices. Turn strips over and roast an additional 30 minutes, again basting twice.

Advance preparation: The pork must marinate for at least 5 hours, but may marinate for as long as 2 days. After roasting, it can be stored in the refrigerator for 1 week or frozen for up to 3 months.

Variation: Use pork spareribs (1 to 1½ lb.) in place of pork butt. Have the butcher cut the slab of ribs lengthwise into long strips about 1½″ wide. Cook in the same way for the same length of time. Cut ribs apart to serve.

Serving suggestions: Thinly slice the roast pork and serve as an appetizer. This pork can also be combined with vegetables or bean cake in stir-fry dishes, added to soup or fried rice, or used as a sandwich filling.

HOISIN SAUCE SPARERIBS
(Hoisin Jerng Pai Gwut)

1. Have the butcher cut the slab of spareribs lengthwise into strips 1½" wide. Cut the rib bones apart and trim off fat. Place in a bowl.
2. Add cornstarch to spareribs and mix well.
3. Combine sauce ingredients and mix well.
4. Heat wok and add oil. Add garlic and green onions and stir-fry for 30 seconds over high heat.
5. Add spareribs and stir-fry for 3 minutes.
6. Add sauce mixture. Bring to a boil, cover, reduce heat to medium, and cook for 40 minutes. There should be at least 1 c. of liquid remaining. If not, add chicken stock to make 1 c.
7. Stir in thickener. Cook for 30 seconds. Serve.

Advance preparation: The entire recipe may be prepared in advance and refrigerated. It keeps well for several days.

Variation: Substitute 2 lb. chicken parts for the spareribs. Cook in the same way and for the same length of time.

Serving suggestion: Serve with Cashew Prawns and Scallops and Steamed Rice.

2 lb. pork spareribs
1½ tbsp. cornstarch
2 tbsp. oil
1 tbsp. finely chopped garlic
2 green onions, diced
chicken stock, as needed

Sauce:

1½ c. chicken stock
1 tsp. salt
1 tsp. sugar
1 tbsp. chili paste with garlic
1 tbsp. hoisin sauce
1 tbsp. catsup
1 tbsp. dark soy sauce
1 tbsp. oyster sauce
1½ tbsp. white wine

Thickener:

1 tbsp. cornstarch, mixed well with 2 tbsp. cold water

Serves 6

KING DU PORK
(King Du Gee Yuk)

1 lb. lean pork loin or butt
egg white from 1 large egg
3 c. oil for deep-frying
¾ c. cornstarch

Seasoning:

½ tsp. salt
½ tsp. sugar
1 tsp. thin soy sauce
1 tsp. oyster sauce

Sauce:

¼ c. water
3½ tbsp. cider vinegar
3 tbsp. catsup
¼ c. sugar
1 tsp. Worcestershire sauce

Thickener:

½ tbsp. cornstarch, mixed well with 1
   tbsp. cold water

Serves 4

1. Trim fat from pork. Cut pork into 1½″ cubes. Place in a bowl.
2. Add seasoning ingredients to pork and mix well. Add egg white and mix well again.
3. Combine ingredients for sauce in a small pan. Bring to a boil. Add thickener and boil for 30 seconds. Remove from heat.
4. Heat oil in wok to 325 degrees. Immediately before frying, add cornstarch to pork cubes and mix well. Drop pork cubes, one at a time, into hot oil. Deep-fry for about 4 minutes. Remove and place on paper towels to drain. Place pork cubes on serving platter.
5. Meanwhile, return sauce to a boil and pour over pork. Serve immediately.

Advance preparation: Steps 1–3 may be done a few hours in advance and kept at room temperature.

PIGS' FEET IN VINEGAR SAUCE
(Sheun Gee Gurk)

1. Have the butcher chop each foot into 6 equal pieces.
2. Bring water to a boil in a large pot. Add pigs' feet and boil for 7 minutes. Drain feet, rinse in cold water, and drain again. Use a small knife to scrape feet pieces clean of any residue. Sprinkle the pieces with salt.
3. Peel ginger and cut into thin slices.
4. In a large enamel pot, bring black and cider vinegars to a boil. Add sugar bars and bring to a boil again, stirring to dissolve sugar.
5. Add ginger and pigs' feet. Cover and cook for 40 minutes, stirring occasionally, over medium heat.
6. Meanwhile, hard-cook the eggs. Immerse in cold water and peel off shells. Add the eggs to the pigs' feet and cook 20 minutes longer.
7. Serve the pigs' feet in individual bowls with a small amount of the sauce.

Advance preparation: This dish can be prepared completely and stored for up to 2 weeks in the refrigerator. Reheat for 10 minutes over medium heat.

Note: For centuries, the Chinese have believed that new mothers regain their strength and vigor by eating this dish. In the past, as the expected birth date approached, friends and relatives would gather at the home of the mother-to-be. They would all participate in the preparation of the pigs' feet and would, of course, all partake of the cooked delicacy. In time, this practice evolved into a tradition, and any visitors who came to see a new baby would always be welcomed with a bowl of the pigs' feet. Today, if someone says, "Invite me over for pigs' feet soon," it is a polite way of saying, "I hope you will soon have a family."

5 lb. pigs' feet
2 qt. water
1 tsp. salt
¾ lb. ginger root*
2 bottles (24 oz. each) Chinese black vinegar**
½ c. cider vinegar
1 lb. Chinese brown sugar bars
8 eggs

*Young ginger is found in Chinese markets during the summer months. It is more tender and has a milder flavor than the older ginger commonly available. Use it for this dish if you can find it. If you can't, regular ginger will work fine.

**This thick, deep-colored vinegar can be found in Chinese markets.

Serves 8

STEAMED PORK AND CHINESE SAUSAGE CAKES
(Gee Yuk Behng)

1 Chinese pork sausage
4 fresh or canned water chestnuts, or 2
    tbsp. finely chopped jicama
½ lb. ground lean pork
1 green onion, finely chopped

Seasoning:

1 tsp. salt
½ tsp. sugar
1 tsp. thin soy sauce
¾ tsp. oyster sauce
1 tbsp. cornstarch

Serves 4

1. Cut sausage into fine pieces.
2. If using fresh water chestnuts, peel and removed and discard top and root ends. Finely chop fresh or canned water chestnuts.
3. Combine sausage, ground pork, green onion, and water chestnuts or jicama on chopping board. With a cleaver, mix and chop for 30 strokes. Place in a shallow dish.
4. Add seasoning ingredients to meat mixture and mix well. Flatten into a patty about 1″ thick.
5. Steam for 20 minutes.

Advance preparation: Steps 1–4 may be completed a few hours in advance and refrigerated. Steam just before serving.

PORK WITH LOTUS ROOT
(Lin Ngau Chow Gee Yuk)

1. Cut pork or chicken into thin strips 1″ by ¼″. Place in a bowl.
2. Add seasoning ingredients to pork or chicken and mix well.
3. Soak black fungus for 15 minutes in warm water to cover. Drain, rinse thoroughly, and drain again. Remove and discard stems. Cut into 1″ slivers; you should have about ½ c.
4. Remove tips from snow peas. Cut each pea in half on the diagonal.
5. Peel celery. Cut into 1½″-long pieces. Cut each piece lengthwise into strips, julienne style.
6. Peel lotus root. Cut into thin slices, then cut each slice in half.
7. Combine thickener ingredients and set aside.
8. Heat wok and add 1 tbsp. oil. Add snow peas, celery, and black fungus and stir-fry for 2 minutes over high heat, sprinkling with salt and sugar. Remove and set aside.
9. Heat wok and add 2 tbsp. oil. Add pork or chicken and stir-fry for 2 minutes over high heat.
10. Add lotus root and chicken stock. Cover and cook for 2 minutes.
11. Add snow pea mixture. Mix thoroughly.
12. Stir in thickener. Cook for 30 seconds. Serve.

Advance preparation: Steps 1–10 may be completed a few hours in advance and kept at room temperature.

½ lb. lean pork butt or skinned and
   boned chicken meat
3 pieces dried black fungus
20 snow peas
1 stalk celery
¼ lb. lotus root
3 tbsp. oil
pinch of salt
pinch of sugar
½ c. chicken stock

Seasoning:

¼ tsp. salt
¼ tsp. sugar
½ tsp. thin soy sauce
1 tsp. oyster sauce
1 tsp. cornstarch

Thickener:

1 tbsp. cornstarch, mixed well with 2
   tbsp. cold water
1 tsp. dark soy sauce
2 tsp. sesame oil

Serves 3

PORK WITH STRING BEANS

(Dow Gawk Gee Yuk)

¾ lb. lean pork butt
1 lb. string beans
1 qt. water
3 tbsp. plus 2 tsp. oil
1 tbsp. hot bean sauce
2 tsp. finely chopped garlic
½ c. chicken stock
¼ tsp. salt
¼ tsp. sugar

Seasoning:

½ tsp. salt
½ tsp. sugar
1 tsp. thin soy sauce
dash of pepper
1 tsp. cornstarch

Thickener:

2 tsp. cornstarch, mixed well with 2
    tsp. cold water

Serves 6

1. Trim fat from pork. Cut pork into strips 1″ by ¼″. Place in a bowl.
2. Add seasoning ingredients to pork. Mix well.
3. Remove tips and strings from string beans. Cut each bean into 4 pieces on the diagonal.
4. Bring water to a boil in a saucepan. Add beans and 2 tsp. oil (the oil helps to keep the beans a vibrant green). Cook, uncovered, for 7 minutes, or until beans are barely tender.
5. Mash hot bean sauce to a paste. Add garlic.
6. Heat wok and add 2 tbsp. oil. Add pork and stir-fry for 2 minutes over high heat. Add ¼ c. chicken stock, cover, and cook for 2 minutes. Remove from wok and set aside.
7. Heat wok and add 1 tbsp. oil. Add bean sauce mixture and string beans. Stir-fry for 2 minutes. Add salt, sugar, and ¼ c. chicken stock. Bring quickly to a boil.
8. Add pork and stir in thickener. Cook for 1 minute. Serve.

Advance preparation: Steps 1–6 may be completed a few hours in advance and kept at room temperature.

SPARERIBS IN BLACK BEAN SAUCE
(See Jup Pai Gwut)

1. Have the butcher cut the slab of spareribs lengthwise into strips 1½″ wide. Cut the rib bones apart and trim off fat.
2. Bring water to a boil, add spareribs, and parboil for 3 minutes. Remove from the heat and drain well.
3. Rinse and drain black beans twice. Mash to a paste with the butt end of a cleaver.
4. Combine sauce ingredients and mix well.
5. Heat wok and add oil. Add garlic and spareribs and stir-fry for 3 minutes over high heat.
6. Add black-bean mixture, sauce mixture, and green onion. Mix thoroughly. Quickly bring to a boil, cover, reduce heat to medium, and cook for 40 minutes. Check occasionally. There should be at least 1 c. of liquid remaining. If not, add chicken stock to make 1 c.
7. Stir in thickener. Cook for 1 minute. Serve.

Advance preparation: The entire recipe may be prepared in advance. Reheat for 7–8 minutes before serving. This dish will still taste delicious the second or third day.

Variations:

   Substitute 2 lb. chicken parts for the spareribs. Omit the parboiling. Reduce chicken stock to 1 c. and reduce cooking time in step 6 to 20 minutes.

   Substitute 1 lb. medium-sized prawns, shelled and deveined, or flank steak, thinly sliced, for the spareribs. Omit the parboiling. Reduce chicken stock to ½ c. and reduce cooking time in step 6 to 5 minutes.

2 lb. pork spareribs
2 qt. water
2½ tbsp. salted black beans
2 tbsp. oil
1 tbsp. finely chopped garlic
1 green onion, chopped
chicken stock, as needed

Sauce:

1½ c. chicken stock
½ tsp. salt
1 tsp. sugar
1 tbsp. thin soy sauce
2 tbsp. oyster sauce

Thickener:

2 tbsp. cornstarch, mixed well with 2 tbsp. cold water

Serves 6

SWEET-AND-SOUR PORK
(Tim Sheun Yuk)

1¼ lb. lean pork butt or pork spareribs
3 stalks celery
½ medium-sized yellow onion
1 bell pepper
3 c. oil for deep-frying
6 tbsp. cornstarch
1 tbsp. oil for stir-frying
pinch of salt
pinch of sugar
1 can (4 oz.) chunk-style pineapple,
    drained and juice reserved for sauce

Marinade:

1 tsp. salt
¼ tsp. sugar
1 tsp. thin soy sauce
1 egg white

Sauce:

¾ c. water
¼ tsp. salt
½ c. sugar
⅓ c. cider vinegar
2½ tbsp. catsup
½ tsp. thin soy sauce
½ c. pineapple juice reserved from
    canned pineapple

Thickener:

2 tbsp. cornstarch, mixed well with 2
    tbsp. cold water

Serves 6

1. Trim fat from pork butt. Cut pork into 1″ cubes. If using spareribs, have the butcher cut the slab lengthwise in 1″ strips. Cut the rib bones apart and trim off all fat. Place meat in a bowl.
2. Add marinade ingredients to pork and mix well. Marinate for 1 hour at room temperature. (If you are short of time, add marinade ingredients but move on directly to the next step.)
3. Peel celery. Cut into 1½″-long pieces. Cut each piece lengthwise into strips, julienne style.
4. Cut onion into wedges ¼″ thick.
5. Cut bell pepper in half and remove and discard seeds. Cut into strips 1″ by ¼″.
6. Heat 3 c. oil in wok to 325 degrees. Immediately before frying, coat marinated pork with cornstarch. Add pork, a piece at a time, to hot oil. Deep-fry for 7 minutes. Remove and drain on paper towels. Remove oil from wok.
7. Heat wok and add 1 tbsp. oil. Add onion, celery, and bell pepper and stir-fry for 2 minutes over high heat, sprinkling with salt and sugar. Remove from wok and set aside.
8. Combine the sauce ingredients in the wok, mix well, and bring to a boil.
9. Stir in thickener. Cook for 1 minute.
10. Add celery mixture, pork, and pineapple. Bring quickly to a boil. Immediately turn off heat. Serve.

Advance preparation: The sauce (step 8) may be made well in advance, omitting the pineapple juice and thickener. Stored in a closed container in the refrigerator, it will keep for 2–3 months. Add pineapple juice and thickener when reheating. Steps 1–7 may be completed a few hours in advance and kept at room temperature.

TWICE-COOKED PORK
(Hui Waw Yuk)

1. Cut pork in half lengthwise.
2. Bring water to a boil in a saucepan. Add ginger, star anise, salt, sugar, white wine, and pork. Cover and cook for 15 minutes over high heat. Remove meat and let cool. Discard liquid.
3. Cut cooked pork into slices about 1½" long by ½" wide.
4. Remove and discard seeds from green and red peppers. Cut into pieces 1½" by ½".
5. Prepare the sauce. Mash bean sauce to a paste. Add remaining sauce ingredients and mix well.
6. Heat wok and add oil. Add garlic and pork and stir-fry for 1 minute over high heat.
7. Add sauce mixture. Stir-fry for 1 minute.
8. Add chicken stock, green onions, and green and red bell peppers. Bring quickly to a boil and cook for 1 minute,
9. Stir in thickener. Cook for 30 seconds. Serve.

Advance preparation: The pork may be cooked (steps 1 and 2) 2 days in advance and refrigerated. Steps 4–8 can be completed several hours in advance and kept at room temperature.

Variations: Substitute 30 snow peas, tips removed and cut into ½" pieces on the diagonal, or 1 c. sliced zucchini for the green bell pepper. Substitute 1 c. thinly sliced carrot for the red bell pepper.

1¼ lb. lean pork butt or loin
3 c. water
1 slice ginger root (about 1" thick and 1" in diameter), peeled and crushed
2 whole star anise
1 tsp. salt
1 tsp. sugar
1 tbsp. white wine
½ green bell pepper
½ red bell pepper
2 tbsp. oil
1 tbsp. finely chopped garlic
½ c. chicken stock
2 green onions, slivered

Sauce:

1½ tbsp. hot bean sauce
2 tsp. sugar
1 tsp. thin soy sauce
1 tbsp. sesame oil
1 tbsp. oyster sauce

Thickener:

2 tsp. cornstarch, mixed well with 1 tbsp. cold water

Serves 4

FISH AND SHELLFISH

ABALONE IN OYSTER SAUCE
(Ho Yau Bau Yeu)

1 can (15 oz.) abalone*
½ c. chicken stock
2 green onions, slivered

Thickener:

1 tbsp. cornstarch, mixed well with 2
*   tbsp. cold water*
1½ tbsp. oyster sauce
1 tsp. sesame oil
½ tsp. sugar

*Be sure to buy expensive abalone; it
will run about $11 per can. Do not
purchase cheap abalone or cans
marked "abalonelike shellfish."

Serves 4

1. Drain abalone. Cut across the grain into very thin slices.
2. Combine thickener ingredients and mix well.
3. Bring chicken stock to a boil.
4. Stir in thickener. Cook for 30 seconds.
5. Add abalone and green onions. Heat only long enough to warm abalone (about 30 seconds), as it will become tough if overcooked. Serve at once.

Advance preparation: Step 1 may be done 1 day in advance and refrigerated.

Variation: Use fresh abalone instead of canned. Cut into thin slices. Pound to tenderize. Increase cooking time to 1 minute.

CASHEW PRAWNS AND SCALLOPS
(Yiu Gwoh Ha Tai Gee)

1. If using raw cashews, toast in a 325-degree oven until golden brown (about 15 minutes).
2. Shell, devein, wash, and drain prawns. Place in a bowl.
3. Cut scallops into pieces about 1½" by ½". Add to bowl with prawns.
4. Add seasoning ingredients to prawns and scallops. Mix well.
5. Peel celery. Cut into 1½"-long pieces. Cut each piece lengthwise into strips, julienne style.
6. Peel carrot. Cut into thin slices on the diagonal.
7. Cut green onions into ½" pieces.
8. Slice mushrooms.
9. Combine thickener ingredients and mix well.
10. Heat wok and add 1½ tbsp. oil. Add mushrooms, carrot, celery, and green onions and stir-fry for 1 minute over high heat. Remove from wok and set aside.
11. Heat wok and add 2 tbsp. oil. Add prawns and scallops and stir-fry for 2 minutes over high heat.
12. Add vegetable mixture and stir well.
13. Stir in thickener. Cook for 30 seconds. Remove from heat.
14. Mix in cashew nuts. Serve.

Advance preparation: Step 1 may be done 2 weeks in advance; store at room temperature in a covered container. Steps 2–10 may be completed a few hours in advance and kept at room temperature.

Serving suggestion: Serve this dish in a deep-fried taro basket (following recipe). Delightful.

1 c. raw cashew nuts or unsalted toasted cashew nuts
½ lb. medium-sized prawns in the shell
½ lb. fresh scallops
2 stalks celery
1 carrot
2 green onions
6 oz. fresh mushrooms
3½ tbsp. oil

Seasoning:

½ tsp. salt
½ tsp. sugar
1 tsp. thin soy sauce
1 tbsp. white wine
2 tsp. cornstarch
dash of pepper

Thickener:

¼ c. chicken stock
1 tbsp. cornstarch
1 tbsp. dark soy sauce
1 tbsp. oyster sauce
1 tbsp. sesame oil
1 tsp. sugar

Serves 4

TARO BASKET
(Jurk Chow)

¾ lb. taro root*
½ tbsp. cornstarch
1½ qt. oil

*Taro is sold in Asian markets in a considerable range of sizes. Buy those about the size of a baking potato, if you can find them. Potatoes may be substituted, but the basket will not be as crispy.

Makes 1 8″ basket

1. Peel taro root.
2. Cut taro into julienne-style strips about 1½″ long and less than ¼″ thick. Place in a bowl.
3. Add cornstarch to strips. Toss to coat well.
4. Spray a standard kitchen strainer (about 8″ in diameter and 4″ deep) with a release agent (the same product that gives skillets a nonstick surface). Spread taro mixture inside the strainer as evenly as possible, to within ½″ of the rim.
5. Heat oil in wok to 325 degrees. Place strainer containing the taro root in oil. You will need to hold the taro strips down with a spoon at first, or they will float in the hot oil. Deep-fry until golden brown (about 4 minutes).
6. Let taro basket cool before removing from strainer. The basket will fall apart if not allowed to cool first.

Advance preparation: Deep-fry the basket a few days in advance and keep in an airtight container at room temperature.

Serving suggestion: This taro basket may be filled with almost any stir-fry dish for a special presentation.

CLAMS IN BLACK BEAN SAUCE
(See Juk Hin)

1. Wash clams thoroughly in cold water. Drain.
2. Bring water to a boil; add clams and cook, uncovered, for about 5 minutes, or until the clams open. Discard any clams that do not open. Drain.
3. Rinse and drain black beans twice. Mash to a paste with the butt of a cleaver. Add garlic.
4. Combine sauce ingredients and mix well.
5. Heat wok and add oil. Add black-bean mixture and clams and stir-fry for 2 minutes over high heat.
6. Add sauce mixture to clams and bring quickly to a boil. Cook just until clams open.
7. Stir in thickener. Cook for 30 seconds. Serve.

Advance preparation: This recipe may be cooked a few hours in advance and kept at room temperature. Reheat for 2 minutes just before serving.

2½ lb. clams in the shell
2 qt. water
1½ tbsp. salted black beans
2 tsp. finely chopped garlic
1½ tbsp. oil

Sauce:

½ c. chicken stock
1 tbsp. sugar
1 tbsp. white wine
1 tbsp. dark soy sauce
1 tbsp. oyster sauce

Thickener:

1½ tsp. cornstarch, mixed well with 1 tbsp. cold water

Serves 4

CURRIED PRAWNS
(Gah-Li Ha)

½ lb. medium-sized prawns in the
   shell
½ medium-sized yellow onion
2 tbsp. oil
1 tbsp. curry powder
1 green onion, finely chopped
⅓ c. chicken stock

Seasoning:

¼ tsp. salt
¼ tsp. sugar
½ tsp. thin soy sauce
1 tsp. oyster sauce
1 tsp. cornstarch

Serves 4

1. Shell, devein, wash, and drain prawns. Place in a bowl.
2. Add seasoning ingredients to prawns. Mix well.
3. Cut yellow onion into wedges ¼" thick.
4. Heat wok and add oil. Add curry powder, yellow and green onions, and prawns and stir-fry for 2 minutes over high heat.
5. Add chicken stock. Cover and cook for 2 minutes over high heat. Serve.

Advance preparation: Steps 1–4 may be completed a few hours in advance and kept at room temperature.

Serving suggestion: Serve over rice as a one-plate meal or with Beef with Oyster Sauce and Steamed Rice for dinner.

DEEP-FRIED PRAWNS
(Jow Ha)

½ lb. medium-sized prawns in the shell
1 tsp. thin soy sauce
2 c. oil for deep-frying

Batter:

½ c. cornstarch
¾ tsp. baking soda
½ tbsp. baking powder
¼ c. plus 2 tbsp. cold water

Condiments:

1 tbsp. mustard powder, mixed with 2
   tbsp. cold water
catsup

Serves 4

1. Mix together batter ingredients. Let stand for at least 5 hours, or as long as overnight at room temperature.
2. Shell, devein, wash, and drain prawns. Place in a bowl.
3. Add soy sauce to prawns. Mix well.
4. Heat oil in wok to 325 degrees. Stir batter. Dip each prawn into batter, then let excess batter drip back into bowl. Immediately drop prawn into hot oil, stirring slightly to keep it from sticking to pan bottom. Deep-fry for 3 minutes. Remove and drain on paper towels.
5. Serve at once with mustard and catsup for dipping.

Advance preparation: Make the batter 1 day in advance and refrigerate.

RED PEPPER PRAWNS
(Laht Jiu Ha)

1. If using raw peanuts, toast in a 325-degree oven until golden brown (about 15 minutes). When cool, chop finely.
2. Shell, devein, wash, and drain prawns. (If using large prawns, cut in half lengthwise.) Place in a bowl.
3. Add seasoning ingredients to prawns. Mix well.
4. Peel celery. Cut into 1½"-long pieces. Cut each piece lengthwise into strips, julienne style.
5. Cut bell pepper in half and remove and discard seeds. Cut into pieces 1" by ¼".
6. Combine thickener ingredients and mix well.
7. Heat wok and add oil. Add chili pepper, prawns, celery, and bell pepper and stir-fry for 3 minutes over high heat.
8. Stir in thickener. Cook for 30 seconds.
9. Remove to serving platter and sprinkle with peanuts. Serve.

Advance preparation: Peanuts may be toasted up to 2 weeks in advance and kept in a closed container at room temperature. Steps 2–7 may be done a few hours ahead and kept at room temperature.

¼ c. raw peanuts or unsalted roasted peanuts
1 lb. medium-sized prawns in the shell
1 stalk celery
1 red bell pepper (green may be substituted)
2 tbsp. oil
½ tsp. crushed dried red chili pepper

Seasoning:

½ tsp. salt
½ tsp. sugar
2 tsp. cornstarch
white from 1 medium-sized egg

Thickener:

½ c. chicken stock
1 tbsp. cornstarch
1 tbsp. white wine
1 tbsp. sesame oil
1 tbsp. oyster sauce

Serves 4

PRAWNS A LA SZECHUAN
(See Chuen Ha)

1 lb. medium-sized prawns in the shell
½ tsp. salt
1 tbsp. cornstarch
2½ tbsp. oil
1½ tbsp. finely chopped garlic*
1 tsp. finely chopped ginger root
2 green onions, finely chopped

Sauce:

2 tsp. cornstarch
⅓ c. chicken stock
2 tbsp. white wine
1½ tbsp. hoisin sauce
1 tsp. chili paste with garlic*
2 tbsp. catsup
1 tbsp. sesame oil
1 tbsp. oyster sauce
2 tsp. sugar

*This amount makes a moderately spicy sauce. Increase or decrease it to taste.

Serves 4

1. Shell, devein, wash, and drain prawns. Place in a bowl.
2. Add salt and cornstarch to prawns. Mix well.
3. Prepare sauce by adding cornstarch to chicken stock and stirring to combine. Add remaining ingredients and mix well.
4. Heat wok and add oil. Add garlic, ginger, and prawns and stir-fry over high heat for 2 minutes.
5. Add sauce and bring quickly to a boil. Cook, uncovered, for 1 minute over high heat.
6. Sprinkle chopped green onions on top. Serve immediately.

Advance preparation: Steps 1–3 may be done a few hours in advance and kept at room temperature.

Variations: You may substitute 1 lb. fresh scallops, red snapper fillets, rock cod fillets, or squid for the prawns. Cut scallops in half, snapper or cod into pieces 1½" by ½", and squid as described in Cutting Techniques section. Cook all of these variations for the same amount of time as the prawns.

Serving suggestion: Serve with Mo Shu Chicken with Mandarin Pancakes, Pot Stickers, and Steamed Rice.

PRAWNS IN BLACK BEAN SAUCE
(See Jup Ha)

1. Shell, devein, wash, and drain prawns. (If using large prawns, cut in half lengthwise.) Place in a bowl.
2. Add seasoning ingredients to prawns. Mix well.
3. Rinse and drain black beans twice. Mash to a paste with the butt of a cleaver. Add chili pepper.
4. Combine thickener ingredients and mix well.
5. Heat wok and add oil. Add garlic and stir-fry for 30 seconds over high heat. Add black-bean mixture and prawns. Stir-fry for 2 minutes over high heat.
6. Stir in thickener and green onion. Cook for 1 minute. Serve.

Advance preparation: Steps 1–3 may be done the night before and refrigerated. Step 4 may be done several hours in advance and kept at room temperature.

1 lb. medium-sized prawns in the shell
2½ tbsp. salted black beans
½ tsp. crushed dried red chili pepper*
1½ tbsp. oil
2 tsp. finely chopped garlic
1 green onion, finely chopped

*This amount makes a moderately spicy dish. Increase or decrease it to taste.

Seasoning:

½ tsp. salt
½ tsp. sugar
1 tsp. thin soy sauce
2 tsp. cornstarch
dash of pepper

Thickener:

¼ c. chicken stock
1 tbsp. cornstarch
1 tbsp. white wine
1 tbsp. sesame oil
1 tbsp. oyster sauce

Serves 4

Prawns with Asparagus
(Ha Lee Sum)

1 lb. medium-sized prawns in the shell
1 green onion, slivered
1¼ lb. fresh asparagus
1½ tbsp. salted black beans
1½ tsp. finely chopped garlic
½ tsp. crushed dried red chili pepper
   (optional)
3 tbsp. oil
¼ tsp. salt
¼ tsp. sugar
¾ c. chicken stock

Seasoning:

¼ tsp. salt
¼ tsp. sugar
2 tsp. white wine
1 tsp. thin soy sauce
1 tbsp. oyster sauce
1 tbsp. cornstarch

Thickener:

2 tsp. cornstarch, mixed well with 1½
   tbsp. cold water
1 tbsp. sesame oil

Serves 4

1. Shell, devein, wash, and drain prawns. Place in a bowl.
2. Add seasoning ingredients to prawns. Mix well. Toss in green onion.
3. Break off and discard the tough base end of asparagus. Cut each spear on the diagonal into slices ½″ thick.
4. Rinse and drain black beans twice. Mash to a paste with the butt of a cleaver. Add garlic and chili pepper.
5. Heat wok and add 1½ tbsp. oil. Add prawns and stir-fry for 2 minutes over high heat. Remove from wok and set aside.
6. Heat wok and add 1½ tbsp. oil. Add black-bean mixture and stir-fry for 30 seconds over high heat.
7. Add asparagus and stir-fry for 2 minutes over high heat. Add salt, sugar, and chicken stock. Bring quickly to a boil and cook, uncovered, for 2 minutes.
8. Add prawns and mix well.
9. Stir in thickener. Cook for 30 seconds. Serve.

Advance preparation: Steps 1–7 may be done a few hours in advance and kept at room temperature.

Variations:
   Substitute 1¼ lb. broccoli or bok choy for the asparagus. See Cutting Techniques section for directions on preparing them. Cook for the same amount of time as the asparagus.
   Substitute 1 lb. fresh scallops, cut in half, for the prawns. Use the same cooking time.

PRAWNS WITH CHINESE LONG BEANS
(Dow Gok Chow Ha Kau)

1. Cut tips off long beans. Cut beans into 2″ lengths.
2. Shell, devein, wash, and drain prawns. Place in a bowl.
3. Add seasoning ingredients to prawns. Mix well.
4. Mash hot bean sauce to a paste.
5. Heat wok and add 1 tbsp. oil. Add prawns and stir-fry for 2 minutes. Remove from wok and set aside.
6. Heat wok and add 1 tbsp. oil. Add bean sauce and long beans and stir-fry for 3 minutes over high heat.
7. Add salt, sugar, and chicken stock. Cover and cook for 4 minutes. Test beans to make sure they are done. If not, cook 1–2 minutes longer.
8. Add prawns and mix well.
9. Stir in thickener ingredients. Cook for 30 seconds. Serve.

Advance preparation: Steps 1–7 may be completed a few hours in advance and kept at room temperature.

½ lb. long beans*
½ lb. medium-sized prawns in the shell
2 tsp. hot bean sauce
2 tbsp. oil
¼ tsp. salt
½ tsp. sugar
¾ c. chicken stock

Seasoning:

½ tsp. salt
½ tsp. sugar
1 tsp. thin soy sauce
dash of pepper

Thickener:

1 tbsp. cornstarch mixed well with 2 tbsp. cold water
1 tsp. sesame oil

*String beans may be substituted. They may need longer cooking in step 6.

Serves 4

STEAMED PRAWNS WITH BLACK BEANS
(See Jup Jing Ha)

¾ lb. medium-sized prawns in the shell
2 tsp. cornstarch
1¼ tbsp. salted black beans
½ tsp. salt
1 tsp. sugar
1½ tsp. thin soy sauce
1 tsp. white wine
1 tsp. oyster sauce
1 tbsp. oil
1 tbsp. finely chopped garlic
1 green onion, chopped

Serves 4

1. Shell, devein, wash, and drain prawns. Place in a shallow dish or pie plate. Add cornstarch and mix well.
2. Rinse and drain black beans twice. Mash to a paste with the butt of a cleaver. Add salt, sugar, soy sauce, white wine, and oyster sauce. Mix well.
3. Pour mixture over prawns and mix well.
4. Add oil, garlic, and green onion. Toss.
5. Steam for 10 minutes.

Advance preparation: Steps 1–4 may be completed a few hours in advance and refrigerated.

Shrimp Cake with Bok Choy

(Ha Behng Bok Choy)

1. Shell, devein, wash, and drain prawns.
2. If using fresh water chestnuts, peel and remove and discard top and root ends. Chop fresh or canned water chestnuts fine.
3. Combine prawns, water chestnuts or jicama, and green onion on cutting board. Chop and mix with cleaver until mixture has a fine texture. (This step may be done in a food processor.) Place in a bowl.
4. Sprinkle seasoning ingredients on prawn mixture and mix well. Add beaten egg and mix well again.
5. Break branches off center stalk of bok choy. Trim ends where they joined the stalk; remove and discard any flowers. Peel tough skin off stalk. Cut leaves, stems, and stalk into 2" pieces on the diagonal.
6. Heat frying pan (preferably one with a nonstick coating or made of cast iron) and add 3 tbsp. oil. Pan-fry prawn mixture for 2 minutes. Turn and flatten into a patty ½" thick. Cook 2 minutes more. Remove from pan and let cool. Cut into strips 1" by ½".
7. Combine thickener ingredients and mix well.
8. Heat wok and add 1½ tbsp. oil. Add bok choy and stir-fry for 2 minutes over high heat. Add salt, sugar, and chicken stock. Bring quickly to a boil. Cook, uncovered, for 2 minutes.
9. Stir in thickener. Cook for 30 seconds.
10. Add shrimp strips and mix well. Cook for 30 seconds. Serve.

Advance preparation: Steps 1–7 may be done a few hours ahead and kept at room temperature.

½ lb. medium-sized prawns in the shell
3 fresh or canned water chestnuts, or 1 tbsp. finely chopped jicama
1 green onion, finely chopped
1 medium-sized egg, lightly beaten
1 lb. bok choy
4½ tbsp. oil
½ tsp. salt
½ tsp. sugar
½ c. chicken stock

Seasoning:

¼ tsp. salt
½ tsp. thin soy sauce
½ tsp. oyster sauce
1½ tbsp. cornstarch

Thickener:

1 tbsp. cornstarch, mixed well with 1 tbsp. cold water
2 tsp. dark soy sauce
1 tsp. sesame oil

Serves 4

SPICED PRAWNS
(Laht Ha)

½ lb. medium-sized prawns in the shell
¼ tsp. salt
¼ tsp. sugar
dash of pepper
2 c. oil for deep-frying
1 tbsp. oil for stir-frying
2 tsp. finely chopped garlic

Batter:

egg white from 1 large egg
2½ tbsp. cornstarch
¼ tsp. baking soda
½ tsp. baking powder
1 tbsp. cold water

Sauce:

1½ tbsp. thin soy sauce
2 tsp. cider vinegar
1 tbsp. sesame oil
1 tbsp. plus 1 tsp. sugar
1½ tbsp. white wine
¼ tsp. crushed dried red chili pepper

Serves 4

1. To prepare the batter, lightly beat egg white with a fork. Add cornstarch, baking soda, baking powder, and water. Mix thoroughly. Let stand at least 5 hours, or as long as overnight at room temperature.
2. Shell, devein, wash, and drain prawns. Place in a bowl.
3. Add salt, sugar, and pepper to prawns. Mix well.
4. Combine sauce ingredients and mix well.
5. Heat 2 c. oil in wok to 325 degrees. Stir batter. Add prawns to batter and coat thoroughly. Drop prawns, one at a time, into the hot oil, stirring lightly after each addition to make sure they don't stick to pan bottom. Deep-fry for 2 minutes. Remove and drain on paper towels.
6. Heat wok and add 1 tbsp. oil. Add garlic and stir-fry for 30 seconds. Add sauce mixture and bring to a boil.
7. Add prawns and mix thoroughly. Do not overcook. Serve.

Advance preparation: The batter may be made 1 day in advance and refrigerated. Steps 2–5 may be completed a few hours ahead and kept at room temperature.

Variations: Substitute ½ lb. fresh scallops, firm white fish fillets, or skinned and boned chicken meat for the prawns. Cut scallops in half and fish or chicken into pieces 1½″ by ½″. Deep-fry for the same amount of time as the prawns.

KUNG PAO SCALLOPS
(Kung Pao Gong Yau Jee)

1. If using raw peanuts, toast in a 325-degree oven until golden brown (about 15 minutes).
2. Cut scallops into pieces 1" by ½". Place in a bowl.
3. Add seasoning ingredients to scallops. Mix well.
4. Remove tips from snow peas. Cut into ¾" pieces on the diagonal.
5. Combine sauce ingredients and mix well.
6. Heat wok and add oil. Add garlic and stir-fry for 30 seconds over high heat. Add scallops, snow peas, and jicama and stir-fry for 3 minutes over high heat.
7. Add sauce mixture and stir well. Cook, uncovered, for 1 minute.
8. Remove to a serving platter. Sprinkle with peanuts. Serve.

Advance preparation: The peanuts may be toasted (step 1) up to 2 weeks in advance and stored in an airtight container at room temperature. Steps 2–5 may be done a few hours in advance and kept at room temperature.

¾ c. raw peanuts or unsalted roasted peanuts
1 lb. fresh scallops
12 snow peas
3 tbsp. oil
1 tbsp. finely chopped garlic
½ c. shredded jicama

Seasoning:

½ tsp. salt
½ tsp. sugar
1 tbsp. white wine
1 tbsp. cornstarch

Sauce:

1 tbsp. hoisin sauce
1 tbsp. chili paste with garlic
1 tbsp. Japanese rice vinegar
1 tbsp. sugar
1½ tbsp. sesame oil

Serves 4

SQUID WITH SNOW PEAS
(Chow Yau Yeu)

1 lb. squid
25 snow peas
7 fresh or canned water chestnuts, or
   3/4 c. thinly sliced jicama
3 tbsp. oil
1/4 tsp. salt
1/4 tsp. sugar
1 tbsp. slivered ginger root

Seasoning:

1/4 c. chicken stock
1/4 tsp. salt
1/4 tsp. sugar
1 tsp. thin soy sauce

Thickener:

2 tsp. cornstarch, mixed well with 2
   tsp. cold water
2 tsp. dark soy sauce

Serves 4

1. Clean and cut squid according to directions in Cutting Techniques section.
2. Remove tips of snow peas. Cut into 1″ pieces on the diagonal.
3. If using fresh water chestnuts, peel and discard top and root ends. Cut fresh or canned water chestnuts into thin slices.
4. Heat wok and add 1 tbsp. oil. Add snow peas and water chestnuts or jicama and stir-fry for 2 minutes over high heat, sprinkling with salt and sugar. Remove and set aside.
5. Heat wok and add 2 tbsp. oil. Add ginger and squid and stir-fry for 2 minutes over high heat. Add seasoning ingredients.
6. Add cooked vegetables. Mix thoroughly.
7. Stir in thickener. Cook for 30 seconds. Serve.

Advance preparation: Steps 1–4 may be done a few hours in advance and kept at room temperature.

Note: For some inexplicable reason, the Chinese use the phrase *chow yau yeu,* literally, "stir-fried squid," to describe someone who has been discharged by an employer. This is a very polite way of communicating the distasteful fact that someone has lost his or her job. For this reason, the dish is *never* served on an auspicious occasion such as New Year's Day.

JENNIE'S FISH IN GRAVY
(Mun Yeu)

1. Cut fish fillets into pieces about 2″ wide by 4–6″ long. Place in a bowl.
2. Spread seasoning ingredients evenly on fish fillets.
3. Boil mushrooms in water to cover for 10 minutes. Drain, rinse, and squeeze dry. Remove and discard stems. Cut into strips ¼″ thick.
4. Cut bamboo shoot into strips, julienne style.
5. Combine thickener ingredients and mix well.
6. Heat wok and add 1 tbsp. oil. Add mushrooms and bamboo shoot and stir-fry for 2 minutes over high heat. Add chicken stock. Bring quickly to a boil. Add thickener mixture. Cook for 30 seconds. Add pork or ham and green onions. Remove from heat.
7. Put cornstarch in a shallow dish and beaten egg in a second dish. Dip each fish fillet into cornstarch, coating both sides, and then into beaten egg. Shake off excess coating. Again dip fillet into cornstarch, coating both sides. (You may need additional cornstarch to coat all of the fillets.)
8. Heat frying pan (preferably one with a nonstick coating or made of cast iron) and add ¼ c. oil. Add fish and pan-fry for 2 minutes. Turn and fry second side for 2 minutes. (Test for doneness. Thicker fillets may need to be cooked longer.) Remove to serving platter.
9. Meanwhile, reheat sauce mixture (from step 6) to a boil. Pour over fish. Serve.

Advance preparation: Steps 1–6 may be done in advance and kept at room temperature.

1½ lb. sea bass, salmon, rock cod, or red snapper fillets (about ¾″ thick)
10 small Chinese dried black mushrooms
2″ piece bamboo shoot
1 tbsp. oil for stir-frying
1¼ c. chicken stock
⅓ c. sliced barbecued pork or cooked ham
2 green onions, slivered
½ c. cornstarch, or as needed
1 large egg, lightly beaten
¼ c. oil for pan-frying

Seasoning:

½ tsp. salt
½ tsp. sugar
1 tsp. thin soy sauce

Thickener:

1 tbsp. cornstarch, mixed well with 1 tbsp. cold water
1 tbsp. dark soy sauce
1 tbsp. oyster sauce
1 tbsp. white wine

Serves 4

STEAMED SALMON CANTONESE
(Jing Sa-Mon Yeu)

1½ lb. salmon steaks (about 1" thick)
2 green onions, slivered
1 tbsp. slivered ginger root
2 tbsp. Tientsin preserved vegetables,
   rinsed and drained

Seasoning:

1½ tsp. salt
1 tsp. dark soy sauce
2 tsp. thin soy sauce
1½ tsp. white wine
1 tsp. sugar
2 tbsp. oil

Serves 4

1. Place salmon steaks in a shallow dish or pie plate. Sprinkle seasoning ingredients over fish, in order given.
2. Arrange green onions, ginger, and preserved vegetables on top of fish.
3. Steam for 15 minutes.

Advance preparation: Steps 1 and 2 may be completed a few hours in advance and refrigerated.

Note: Steaks or fillets of other types of fish, such as perch, rock cod, sand dab, rex sole, turbot, butterfish, or halibut, may be substituted for the salmon. Vary the cooking time according to the thickness of the pieces. For example, if fish pieces are ½" thick, steam for 10 minutes. Add 5 minutes for each additional ½" of thickness.

Serving suggestion: Serve with Broccoli in Oyster Sauce and Steamed Rice.

STEAMED SAND DABS
(Jing Top Sah Yeu)

2 sand dabs (½ lb. each)
1 tbsp. bean sauce*
½ tsp. salt
½ tsp. sugar
1 tbsp. thin soy sauce
1 tsp. oyster sauce
dash of pepper
2 tsp. slivered ginger root
1 green onion, chopped
1 tbsp. oil

*Szechuan-style hot bean sauce may be used for a spicier dish.

Serves 3

1. Clean and scale sand dabs or have your fishmonger do it. Remove and discard fins and tails. Rinse in cold water and cut each fish crosswise into 3 equal pieces. Place in a shallow dish or pie plate.
2. Mash bean sauce to a paste.
3. Add salt, sugar, soy sauce, oyster sauce, pepper, bean sauce, ginger, green onion, and oil to fish, in that order.
4. Steam for 10 minutes.

Advance preparation: Steps 1–3 may be done several hours in advance and refrigerated.

Serving suggestion: Serve with Cantonese Boiled Chicken, Prawns with Chinese Long Beans, and Steamed Rice for a typical family dinner.

VEGETABLES

ASPARAGUS IN OYSTER SAUCE
(Ho Yau Lee Sun)

1½ lb. asparagus
3 tbsp. oil
1½ qt. water
2½ tbsp. oyster sauce
1 tsp. sesame oil

Serves 4

1. Break off and discard tough base end of asparagus. Cut each spear on the diagonal into ½" pieces.
2. Place 3 tbsp. oil in a small saucepan.
3. Bring water to a boil in another saucepan. Add asparagus and cook, uncovered, for 2 minutes over high heat. (Start timing immediately. Do not wait for water to return to a boil.) Drain.
4. While asparagus are cooking, heat oil for 1 minute over high heat. Place asparagus in a shallow serving dish. Pour hot oil over the vegetable. The oil should be hot enough to sizzle when it hits the asparagus.
5. Pour the oyster sauce and sesame oil over the asparagus. Toss and serve.

Advance preparation: The asparagus may be cut the night before and refrigerated.

Variations: Substitute 1½ lb. broccoli, bok choy, zucchini, swiss chard, or snow peas for the asparagus. See Cutting Techniques section for information on cutting broccoli, bok choy, snow peas, and zucchini. Trim and discard root end of swiss chard; cut leaves and stalks in 1" pieces on the diagonal. Cook broccoli, bok choy, zucchini, and swiss chard for the same amount of time as asparagus. Cook snow peas for only 1 minute.

Note: In step 4, the oil must be at the smoking point. If you are unsure if it is hot enough, drizzle a few drops over the vegetable. If the oil doesn't sizzle, return the remainder of it to the heat.

Bean Sprouts with Mixed Vegetables

(Chow Ngah Choy)

1. Peel celery. Cut into 1½″ pieces. Cut each piece lengthwise into strips, julienne style.
2. Remove seeds from bell pepper. Cut into strips 1″ by ¼″.
3. Combine thickener ingredients and mix well.
4. Heat wok and add oil. Quickly add all vegetables and stir-fry for 2 minutes over high heat.
5. Add salt, sugar, and chicken stock. Bring to a boil.
6. Stir in thickener. Cook for 30 seconds. Serve.

Advance preparation: Steps 1 and 2 may be completed the night before and refrigerated.

2 stalks celery
1 red or green bell pepper
2 green onions, slivered
2 tbsp. oil
1 lb. bean sprouts
½ tsp. salt
½ tsp. sugar
½ c. chicken stock

Thickener:

1 tbsp. cornstarch, mixed well with 2 tbsp. cold water
1 tbsp. dark soy sauce
1 tbsp. sesame oil
1 tbsp. oyster sauce

Serves 6

Chow Bean Cake

(Chow Dow Foo)

1. Drain bean cake and cut into 1″ cubes.
2. Cut barbecued pork into slices about 1″ by ½″ by ¼″.
3. Mash bean sauce to a paste. Add garlic.
4. Heat wok and add oil. Add bean sauce mixture and bean cake and stir-fry for 2 minutes over high heat.
5. Add salt, sugar, soy sauce, oyster sauce, chicken stock, and barbecued pork. Bring to a boil. Cover and cook for 2 minutes over high heat.
6. Add green onions and stir in thickener. Cook for 30 seconds. Serve.

Advance preparation: Steps 1–5 may be completed a few hours in advance and kept at room temperature.

Variations: Substitute ½ lb. medium-sized prawns in the shell, flank steak, or cooked ham for the barbecued pork. See Cutting Techniques section for information on preparing prawns and flank steak. Cut ham into thin slices. If using prawns or beef, stir-fry for 2 minutes in 1 tbsp. oil, then add in step 5.

Serving suggestion: Serve this dish over rice for lunch, or with several other dishes for dinner.

1 package (about 1 lb.) firm bean cake
½ lb. barbecued pork
2 tbsp. hot bean sauce
1 tbsp. finely chopped garlic
1 tbsp. oil
¼ tsp. salt
¼ tsp. sugar
½ tsp. thin soy sauce
1½ tsp. oyster sauce
1 c. chicken stock
2 green onions, slivered

Thickener:

1½ tsp. cornstarch, mixed well with 1 tbsp. water

Serves 5

STUFFED BEAN CAKES
(Yeung Dow Foo)

¼ lb. medium-sized prawns in the shell
8 small Chinese dried black
   mushrooms
½ lb. ground lean pork
1 green onion, chopped
1 package (about 1 lb.) firm bean cake
3 tbsp. oil

Seasoning:

½ tsp. salt
½ tsp. sugar
1 tsp. thin soy sauce
¾ tsp. oyster sauce
dash of pepper
2 tsp. cornstarch

Sauce:

1 tbsp. bean sauce
1 tbsp. thin soy sauce
1 tbsp. white wine
2 tsp. sugar
¾ c. chicken stock

Thickener:

2 tsp. cornstarch, mixed well with 2
   tsp. cold water

Serves 4

1. Shell, devein, wash, and drain prawns. Mince.
2. Boil mushrooms for 10 minutes in water to cover. Drain, rinse, and squeeze dry. Remove and discard stems. Chop into very fine pieces.
3. Place prawns, mushrooms, pork, and green onion on a chopping board. Chop and mix with a cleaver for about 30 strokes. (A food processor may be used for this step.) Place in a bowl.
4. Add seasoning ingredients to prawn mixture. Mix well.
5. Drain bean cake and cut into triangles approximately 3″ on each side and ½″ thick. (How you do this will depend on how the bean cake was cut before packaging. If the bean cake was cut into 4 pieces, the slices are usually already about ½″ thick. Simply cut each slice in half on the diagonal. If the bean cake is in 2 pieces, cut it into 2 layers first, then proceed as above.) Make a pocket by cutting a lengthwise slit in the longest side of each triangle. Carefully scoop a small amount of bean cake from the slit in each triangle to create a pocket. Reserve the removed bean cake for another use.
6. Stuff the pockets with the pork mixture. Set aside.
7. To make the sauce, mash bean sauce to a paste. Add remaining sauce ingredients and mix thoroughly.
8. Heat frying pan (preferably one with a nonstick coating) and add oil. Carefully place stuffed triangles in pan, meat side down. Cook until golden brown (about 2 minutes). Turn and brown top and then bottom sides for about 1 minute each.
9. Transfer browned bean cakes to a wok. Add sauce mixture and bring to a boil. Cover and cook for 3 minutes.
10. Stir in thickener. Cook for 30 seconds. Serve.

Advance preparation: Steps 1–8 may be completed several hours in advance and kept at room temperature.

STEAMED STUFFED BEAN CAKES

(Jing Yeung Dow Foo)

1. Prepare the stuffed bean cakes as described through step 6. Place in a shallow dish or pie plate.
2. Mash bean sauce to a paste. Add soy sauce, oyster sauce, sugar, and pepper and mix well.
3. Cover the bean cakes with the bean sauce mixture.
4. Drizzle oil over bean cakes.
5. Sprinkle green onion on top.
6. Steam for 15 minutes.

12 Stuffed Bean Cakes (preceding)
1 tbsp. bean sauce
2 tsp. thin soy sauce
1 tbsp. oyster sauce
½ tsp. sugar
dash of pepper
1½ tbsp. oil
1 green onion, chopped

Serves 4

STUFFED BEAN CAKES IN BROTH

(Yeung Dow Foo Tong)

1. Prepare the stuffed bean cakes as described through step 6.
2. Cut lettuce into pieces 2" wide.
3. Bring chicken stock to a boil.
4. Add bean cakes and lettuce to stock. Cover and cook for 5 minutes over high heat.
5. Serve with soy sauce.

12 Stuffed Bean Cakes (preceding)
¼ head iceberg lettuce
3 c. chicken stock

Condiment:
about 2 tbsp. thin soy sauce

Serves 4

DEEP-FRIED BEAN CAKES
(Jow Dow Foo)

1 package (about 1 lb.) firm bean cake
2 tbsp. finely chopped cooked ham or
    barbecued pork
2 tbsp. finely chopped green onion
3 c. oil for deep-frying
½ c. chicken stock

Seasoning:

½ tsp. salt
½ tsp. sugar
1 tbsp. white wine
1 tbsp. oyster sauce
3 tbsp. cornstarch

Thickener:

2 tsp. cornstarch, mixed well with 1
    tbsp. cold water
1 tsp. sesame oil
2 tsp. dark soy sauce

Serves 5

1. Drain bean cake well. Place in a bowl. Mash to a paste.
2. Add ham or barbecued pork, green onion, and seasoning ingredients and mix well.
3. Form mixture into 16 egg-shaped pieces.
4. Combine thickener ingredients and mix well.
5. Heat oil in wok to 325 degrees. Drop 8 of the bean-cake ovals into hot oil, one at a time. Deep-fry until golden brown, turning once (about 2 minutes on each side, for a total cooking time of 4 minutes). Remove and drain on paper towels. Place in a 350-degree oven while completing step 6.
6. Deep-fry remaining bean-cake ovals, then arrange all of the ovals on a serving dish.
7. Meanwhile, bring chicken stock to a boil. Stir in thickener. Cook for 30 seconds. Pour over bean cake and serve.

Advance preparation: Steps 1–3 may be done a few hours in advance and kept at room temperature.

SPICED CABBAGE

(Lot Yeh Choy)

1. Cut cabbage into pieces approximately 1½" by ¼".
2. Combine sesame oil, soy sauce, vinegar, sugar, salt, and chili paste with garlic in a bowl. Mix well.
3. Heat wok and add oil. Add cabbage and stir-fry for 2 minutes over high heat.
4. Add sesame-oil mixture and mix well. Remove from the heat and let cool.
5. Chill in the refrigerator for 2 hours before serving.

Advance preparation: The entire dish may be completed in advance and kept in the refrigerator for up to 8 hours.

Serving suggestion: Serve with Cantonese Beef Stew, Red Pepper Prawns, and Steamed Rice for a satisfying dinner.

1 head green cabbage (about 1 lb.)
1 tbsp. sesame oil
1 tbsp. thin soy sauce
1 tbsp. cider vinegar
1 tbsp. sugar
¼ tsp. salt
1 tsp. chili paste with garlic*
1 tbsp. oil

*Omit the chili paste if you don't like spicy food.

Serves 6

SPICED EGGPLANT

(Lot Ker Jee)

1. Cut eggplant on the diagonal into ¼" slices.
2. Combine sauce ingredients and mix well.
3. Heat wok and add 4 tbsp. (¼ c.) oil. Add eggplant and pan-fry about 1½ minutes on each side over medium-high heat. Remove and drain on paper towels.
4. Heat wok and add 1 tbsp. oil. Add garlic and ginger and stir-fry for 30 seconds over high heat. Add eggplant and sauce mixture. Bring to a boil.
5. Stir in thickener. Cook for 30 seconds.
6. Remove to serving platter. Garnish with green onion. Serve.

Advance preparation: This dish may be served hot or cold. Prepare several hours in advance and refrigerate at least 2 hours, or reheat just before serving.

Serving suggestion: Serve with Hot-and-Sour Soup, Cashew Chicken, and Steamed Rice.

6 oz. Oriental eggplant
5 tbsp. oil
1 tsp. finely chopped garlic
1 tsp. finely chopped ginger
1 green onion, finely chopped

Sauce:

⅓ c. chicken stock
1 tsp. chili paste
¼ tsp. salt
¼ tsp. sugar
1 tsp. sesame oil
1 tsp. thin soy sauce
1 tsp. cider vinegar

Thickener:

2 tsp. cornstarch, mixed well with 1 tbsp. cold water

Serves 3

KOHLRABI IN HUNAN SAUCE
(Hunan Gwah Choy)

1 tbsp. raw white sesame seeds
1 lb. kohlrabi
2 tbsp. oil
1 tbsp. finely chopped garlic
1 green onion, finely chopped

Sauce:

1½ tbsp. hot bean sauce
¼ c. chicken stock
1 tbsp. sesame oil
1 tbsp. Japanese rice vinegar
1 tbsp. oyster sauce
1 tbsp. sugar

Thickener:

1 tbsp. cornstarch, mixed well with 2
*   tbsp. cold water*

Serves 4

1. Toast sesame seeds in a dry (no oil) frying pan until golden brown (about 1 minute).
2. Using a sharp knife, remove skin from kohlrabi and discard. Cut in half lengthwise. Cut each half in half again lengthwise, to form quarters. Cut each quarter into slices ¼″ thick; you should have about 2 c.
3. To make the sauce, mash bean sauce to a paste. Add remaining sauce ingredients and mix well.
4. Heat wok and add oil. Add garlic and stir-fry for 30 seconds over high heat. Add kohlrabi and stir-fry for 2 minutes over high heat.
5. Add sauce. Cook, uncovered, for 2 minutes over high heat.
6. Stir in thickener. Cook for 30 seconds.
7. Remove to serving platter. Sprinkle with green onion and sesame seeds. Serve.

MUSHROOMS IN OYSTER SAUCE
(Ho Yau Doong Goo)

1. Soak mushrooms in warm water to cover for 30 minutes. Drain, rinse, and squeeze dry. Cut off and discard stems.
2. Add cornstarch to mushrooms and mix well.
3. Heat wok and add oil. Add mushrooms and stir-fry for 2 minutes over high heat.
4. Add ginger, wine, sugar, and 2 c. chicken stock. Bring quickly to a boil. Cover, reduce heat, and simmer for 1 hour. Stir occasionally to be sure there is sufficient liquid. There should be at least 1 c. of liquid remaining. If not, add chicken stock to make 1 c.
5. Stir in oyster sauce and soy sauce.
6. Stir in thickener. Cook for 1 minute.
7. Remove to platter. Garnish with green onions. Serve.

Advance preparation: The entire recipe, except for the garnish, may be completed a few days in advance and stored in the refrigerator. Reheat to serving temperature and garnish with green onions.

Serving suggestion: Serve with Hoisin Sauce Spareribs and Tomato Beef Chow Mein.

Note: Chinese mushrooms are a very good "company" dish, as they are considered a delicacy. This method of preparation accords to the mushroom the special treatment it deserves.

3 oz. Chinese dried black mushrooms (about 25 small mushrooms)
1 tbsp. cornstarch
2 tbsp. oil
1 piece ginger root (about 1" thick and 1" in diameter), peeled and crushed
1 tbsp. white wine
2 tsp. sugar
2 c. chicken stock, or as needed
2 tbsp. oyster sauce
2 tsp. dark soy sauce
2 green onions, slivered

Thickener:

1 tbsp. cornstarch, mixed well with 2 tbsp. cold water

Serves 5

PICKLED MUSTARD GREENS
(Sheum Guy Choy)

1½ lb. Chinese mustard greens

Pickling Liquid:

1½ c. cold water
¾ c. cider vinegar
1 c. sugar

Makes 1 qt.

1. To make the pickling liquid, bring water, vinegar, and sugar to a boil in an enamel-coated or stainless-steel saucepan, stirring to dissolve sugar. Remove from heat and set aside to cool.
2. Break branches off center stalk of Chinese mustard greens. Cut branches into 2″ pieces on the diagonal. Peel outer covering from center stalk. Cut into 1½″ pieces on the diagonal. Put mustard greens into a 1-qt. jar. They should not be too tightly packed.
3. Pour cooled pickling liquid over mustard greens. (This amount of pickling liquid may not cover the greens completely at first, but by the following day they will have wilted enough to be fully immersed.) Cover and refrigerate for 3 days before eating.

Variations: For a spicier version, add ½ tsp. crushed dried red chili pepper to the pickling mixture. You may also substitute a combination of daikon (Japanese long white radish) and carrot (total weight 1½ lb.) for the mustard greens. Peel the radish and carrot. Cut each into thin slices on the diagonal. Place in a glass jar and proceed as directed in step 3.

Serving suggestion: A small plate of these pickled greens makes a good appetizer or side dish for almost any meal.

HOT PEPPER TOSS
(Laht Jiu Soong)

1. Cut bell pepper and chili peppers in half and remove and discard seeds. Cut peppers into ½″ squares.
2. If using fresh water chestnuts, peel and remove and discard top and root ends. Cut fresh or canned water chestnuts into ½″ cubes.
3. Cut barbecued pork into ½″ cubes.
4. Peel celery. Cut into ½″ cubes.
5. Cut green onions to match other cut vegetables in size as closely as possible.
6. Rinse and drain black beans twice. Mash to a paste with the butt of a cleaver.
7. Heat wok and add oil. Add black beans and stir-fry for 30 seconds over high heat.
8. Add peppers, water chestnuts or jicama, pork, celery, green onions, salt, and sugar. Stir-fry for 2 minutes over high heat.
9. Add chicken stock and cook, uncovered, for 2 minutes over high heat.
10. Stir in thickener. Cook for 30 seconds. Serve.

Advance preparation: The entire recipe may be completed a few hours in advance and kept at room temperature. Reheat in a nonstick frying pan.

Note: This typical home-style dish mates beautifully with the bland taste of rice.

1 medium-sized green bell pepper
2 fresh green or red chili peppers
8 fresh or canned water chestnuts, or
 ½ c. cubed (½″) jicama
½ lb. barbecued pork
2 stalks celery
2 green onions
1 tbsp. salted black beans
2 tbsp. oil
½ tsp. salt
½ tsp. sugar
⅓ c. chicken stock

Thickener:

1 tbsp. cornstarch, mixed well with 2
 tbsp. cold water
1 tbsp. oyster sauce

Serves 5

EGG FOO YUNG

(Foo Yung Dong)

2 tbsp. raw white sesame seeds
½ medium-sized yellow onion
¼ lb. barbecued pork or cooked ham
about 7 tbsp. oil
½ lb. bean sprouts
½ c. sliced canned winter bamboo
  shoots
½ tsp. salt
½ tsp. sugar
6 large eggs
1 tbsp. oyster sauce
1 tsp. thin soy sauce
1 green onion, finely chopped

Gravy:

1 c. chicken stock
⅓ c. sliced fresh mushrooms (optional)
1½ tbsp. cornstarch, mixed well with
  1½ tbsp. cold water
½ tsp. sugar
½ tsp. dark soy sauce

Serves 5

1. Toast sesame seeds in a dry (no oil) frying pan over medium heat until golden brown (about 1 minute).
2. Cut yellow onion into thin slices.
3. Cut pork or ham into thin strips, julienne style.
4. Heat wok and add 1 tbsp. oil. Add bean sprouts, yellow onion, barbecued pork or ham, bamboo shoots, salt, and sugar and stir-fry for 2 minutes over high heat. Do not overcook. Remove from wok and set aside to cool.
5. Make the gravy. In a small saucepan, bring chicken stock and mushrooms to a boil. Combine cornstarch mixture, sugar, and soy sauce and stir into boiling stock. Cook for 1 minute. Keep warm.
6. In a bowl, beat eggs. Add oyster sauce and soy sauce. Mix well.
7. Add the cooled stir-fried ingredients to egg mixture and mix well.
8. Heat a large nonstick frying pan and add 2 tbsp. oil. Add ½ c. of the egg-vegetable mixture to the pan for each pancake. An 11″ pan will hold 4 pancakes. Fry pancakes about 2 minutes on each side. Remove to heatproof serving dish and place in an oven preheated to 300 degrees. Turn off oven heat.
9. Repeat procedure with remaining oil and egg-vegetable mixture. You should make about 10 pancakes in all.
10. Meanwhile, reheat the gravy to serving temperature. Pour hot gravy over patties and garnish with chopped onion and sesame seeds.

Advance preparation: The sesame seeds may be toasted up to 2 weeks in advance (step 1) and kept in an airtight container at room temperature. Steps 2–6 may be done a few hours in advance and kept at room temperature.

Note: These patties (without the gravy) make great sandwich fillings.

CLAY-POT, SIZZLING-PLATTER, AND FIREPOT DISHES

SPARERIBS IN CLAY POT
(Pai Gwut Bow)

1 lb. pork spareribs
2 qt. water
2 green onions, finely chopped

Sauce:

1/4 c. cold water
1 tbsp. white wine
2 tbsp. white or cider vinegar
3 tbsp. sugar
1/4 c. dark soy sauce*

*Dark soy sauce gives rich color and
full flavor to the meat and gravy.

Serves 5

1. Have the butcher cut the slab of spareribs lengthwise into strips 1½" wide. Cut the rib bones apart and trim off excess fat.
2. Bring water to a boil. Add ribs and parboil for 2 minutes. Drain well.
3. Combine sauce ingredients and add to a 9" clay pot or flameproof glass saucepan. Bring to a boil. Add spareribs. Cover and cook for 30 minutes over medium heat. (Check liquid occasionally. There should be ¾ c. sauce remaining at the end of 30 minutes. If there isn't, mix up additional sauce and add it to the pot.)
4. Garnish with green onions. Serve.

Advance preparation: The entire recipe may be prepared a day in advance and reheated on the stove or in a microwave oven. It may also be kept hot in a warm oven for up to 1 hour.

Variations: Substitute 1 lb. chicken for the spareribs. If using thighs or drumsticks, leave whole; cut whole breast into 6 equal pieces on the bone. Beef ribs, cut into 2" pieces, are also delicious cooked this way. Cooking time remains the same for both variations.

SCALLOPS AND PRAWNS IN CLAY POT
(Gong Yau Jee Ha Bow)

1. Shell, devein, wash, and drain prawns. Place in a bowl.
2. Cut scallops in half lengthwise and add to bowl.
3. Add seasoning ingredients to bowl. Mix well.
4. Remove tips from snow peas. Cut on the diagonal into pieces about ½" wide.
5. To make the sauce, mash bean sauce to a paste. Add remaining sauce ingredients and mix well.
6. Heat wok and add oil. Add garlic, scallops, and prawns and stir-fry for 2 minutes over high heat. Remove to clay pot.
7. Add snow peas, jicama, green onions and sauce mixture. Cover and cook for 10 minutes.
8. Stir in thickener. Cook for 30 seconds. Serve.

Advance preparation: Steps 1–7 may be completed a few hours in advance and kept at room temperature. Unlike other clay-pot recipes that may be completed in advance and reheated, this seafood version is better when served immediately.

Variations: You may use all prawns or all scallops. Or substitute 1 lb. firm white fish fillets (rock cod or red snapper), cut into 1" squares, or 1 lb. squid, cleaned and cut into 1½" strips (see Cutting Techniques), for the prawns and scallops. Cooking time remains the same.

½ lb. medium-sized prawns in the shell
½ lb. fresh scallops
20 snow peas
3 tbsp. oil
1 tbsp. finely chopped garlic
½ c. shredded (1½" long) jicama
2 green onions, slivered

Seasoning:

⅓ tsp. salt
⅓ tsp. sugar
1 tsp. thin soy sauce
1 tbsp. cornstarch

Sauce:

1½ tbsp. hot bean sauce
½ c. chicken stock
1 tbsp. oyster sauce
1 tsp. dark soy sauce
1 tbsp. sesame oil
2 tsp. sugar

Thickener:

2 tsp. cornstarch, mixed well with 2 tsp. cold water

Serves 4

BEEF IN CLAY POT
(Ngow Yuk Bow)

1 lb. flank steak
½ can (15 oz.) whole winter bamboo
   shoots
3 pieces dried black fungus
2 tbsp. oil
2 green onions, slivered

Marinade:

½ tsp. baking soda
1 tsp. warm water
½ tsp. salt
½ tsp. sugar
1 tsp. thin soy sauce
1 tbsp. white wine
1 tbsp. oyster sauce
dash of pepper

Sauce:

1 tbsp. bean sauce
1 tbsp. hoisin sauce
½ c. chicken stock

Thickener:

1 tbsp. cornstarch, mixed well with 2
   tbsp. cold water
1 tbsp. sesame oil
1 tbsp. oyster sauce

Serves 4

1. Cut flank steak lengthwise (with grain of meat) into 3 equal strips each about 1½″ wide. Cut each strip across the grain into thin slices. Place in a bowl.
2. To make the marinade, dissolve baking soda in warm water. Add to beef. Sprinkle remaining marinade ingredients on beef. Mix well. Marinate for at least 4 hours or overnight in the refrigerator.
3. Cut bamboo shoots into thin strips, julienne style. You should have about 1 c.
4. Soak fungus in warm water to cover for 15 minutes. Drain, rinse thoroughly, and drain again. Remove and discard stems. Cut into slivers 1″ long; you should have about ½ c.
5. To make the sauce mixture, mash bean sauce to a paste. Add hoisin sauce and chicken stock and mix well.
6. Heat wok and add oil. Add flank steak, bamboo shoots, and fungus and stir-fry for 2 minutes over high heat. Remove to a 9″ clay pot or flameproof glass saucepan.
7. Add sauce mixture and green onion. Cover and cook for 10 minutes over high heat. Stir occasionally to prevent burning.
8. Combine thickener ingredients. Add to pot and cook for 30 seconds. Serve.

Advance preparation: The entire recipe may be prepared in advance and reheated on the stove or in a microwave oven. It will also stay hot in a warm oven for up to 1 hour. The clay pot retains heat very efficiently.

CHICKEN IN CLAY POT
(Gai Bow)

1. Skin and bone chicken. Cut into pieces 1½″ by ½″. Place in a bowl.
2. Add seasoning ingredients to chicken. Mix well.
3. Cut green onions into ½″ pieces.
4. Cut red onion into ¾″ cubes. You should have about ½ c.
5. Cut lettuce into pieces 2″ wide.
6. Rinse and drain black beans twice. Drain and mash to a paste with the butt end of a cleaver. Add garlic.
7. Heat wok and add oil. Add black-bean mixture, green onions, red onion, and chicken and stir-fry for 2 minutes over high heat. Remove from heat.
8. Put lettuce in the bottom of a 9″ clay pot or flameproof glass saucepan. Add stir-fried chicken mixture and mushrooms. Combine sauce ingredients and add to pot. Cover and cook over high heat for 10 minutes, stirring to prevent burning.
9. Combine thickener ingredients and add to pot. Cook for 30 seconds. Serve.

Advance preparation: The entire recipe may be prepared a day in advance and reheated on the stove or in a microwave oven. It will also stay hot in a warm oven for up to 1 hour.

1 whole chicken breast, or 1 lb. chicken thighs
2 green onions
¼ medium-sized red onion
¼ head iceberg lettuce
2 tbsp. salted black beans
2 tsp. finely chopped garlic
2 tbsp. oil
1 can (15 oz.) straw mushrooms, drained and rinsed, or 6 oz. fresh mushrooms

Seasoning:

½ tsp. salt
½ tsp. sugar
1 tsp. thin soy sauce
2 tsp. cornstarch

Sauce:

¼ c. chicken stock
1 tbsp. dark soy sauce
1 tbsp. oyster sauce
1 tbsp. white wine

Thickener:

1 tbsp. cornstarch, mixed well with 2 tbsp. cold water
1 tbsp. sesame oil

Serves 4

CHICKEN AND PRAWN SIZZLING PLATTER

(Tit Behn Gai Tung Ha)

1 whole chicken breast
½ lb. medium-sized prawns in the shell
¼ lb. fresh mushrooms
2 tbsp. oil
1 tbsp. finely chopped garlic
2 tsp. finely chopped ginger root
½ c. chicken stock
2 green onions, slivered

Seasoning for Chicken:

½ tsp. salt
½ tsp sugar
1 tsp. thin soy sauce
1 tbsp. oyster sauce
1 tbsp. white wine
2 tsp. cornstarch

Seasoning for Prawns:

½ tsp. thin soy sauce
1 tsp. cornstarch

Thickener:

1 tbsp. cornstarch, mixed well with 2
   tbsp. cold water
1 tbsp. sesame oil

Serves 5

1. Preheat an 11″ cast-iron sizzling platter or aluminum steak plate in a preheated 500-degree oven for 20 minutes. It is very important to have it very hot.
2. Skin and bone chicken. Cut into pieces 1½″ by ½″. Place in a bowl.
3. Add seasoning ingredients for chicken to bowl. Mix well.
4. Shell, devein, wash, and drain prawns. Place in a bowl.
5. Add seasoning ingredients for prawns to bowl. Mix well.
6. Slice mushrooms.
7. Heat wok and add oil. Add garlic, ginger, and chicken and stir-fry for 2 minutes over high heat.
8. Add chicken stock and prawns. Cover and cook for 2 minutes over high heat.
9. Add mushrooms and green onions. Stir-fry for 1 minute over high heat.
10. Stir in thickener. Cook for 30 seconds. Remove to a dish.
11. Immediately take the hot food and the preheated sizzling platter to the table. Quickly pour the chicken mixture onto the platter. If both the food and the platter are very hot, there will be a loud sizzling noise. Caution: This is a "fun" dish, but along with the sizzle there may be some spattering. If you are entertaining guests and using an elegant tablecloth, you may wish to protect it with plastic. Another solution is to invite the guests to the kitchen "to see the show" before taking the platter to the table.

Advance preparation: Steps 1–9 may be completed a few hours ahead of serving and kept at room temperature. Be sure to allow plenty of time for the platter to get very hot before serving.

Note: Any stir-fry recipe, such as Beef in Oyster Sauce, Mongolian Beef, Cashew Chicken, Red Pepper Prawns, or Kung Pao Scallops, can be served on a sizzling platter.

Mongolian Firepot
(Dah Bien Loo)

1. Skin and bone chicken. Cut into pieces 1″ by ½″. Place in a serving dish.
2. Add seasoning ingredients for chicken to dish. Mix well.
3. Shell, devein, wash, and drain prawns. Place in a serving dish.
4. Place pork in a bowl. Add seasoning ingredients and mix well. Shape into balls 1″ in diameter. Place in a serving dish.
5. Cut green onions into 1″ pieces. Place in a serving dish.
6. Peel celery. Cut into 2″-long pieces. Cut each piece lengthwise into strips, julienne style. Place in a serving dish.
7. Drain bean cake and cut into 1″ cubes. Place in a serving dish.
8. Wash spinach carefully to rid it of sand and grit. Cut off and discard lower ½″ of stems. Cut leaves and tender stems into pieces 2″ wide. Place in a serving bowl.
9. Cut lettuce into pieces 2″ wide. Place in a serving bowl.
10. Pour chicken stock into an electric deep-fryer or a deep electric skillet or wok. Bring to a boil.
11. Combine dipping sauce ingredients and divide among 4 small condiment dishes.
12. Arrange the filled serving dishes around the pot of boiling broth.
13. Provide each guest with a small bowl, 2 pairs of chopsticks (one for handling the food in the firepot and the second for eating), a 2″ Chinese wire strainer, and a dish of dipping sauce.
14. Each person selects the foods of his or her choice and places them in the strainer. The diner then immerses the strainer in the broth until the food is cooked. Thus, each person cooks the foods to suit his or her own taste. Suggested cooking time: celery, spinach, lettuce, green onions, bean cake, and prawns, about 1 minute; chicken and pork balls, about 2 minutes.

Advance preparation: All the meats and vegetables may be readied for cooking a day in advance. Store in the refrigerator.

Note: This dish is a challenge to the imagination. What else might you add to the firepot? Suggestions include thinly sliced flank steak, small pieces of squid, and coarsely shredded Napa cabbage, watercress, or bok choy.

A firepot meal is good party fare because it invites each guest to do his or her own thing. The fun may even begin in the kitchen, with the guests sharing in the preparation of the various ingredients.

When everyone has cooked and eaten enough, ladle the flavorful stock into bowls and serve as a soup course.

This recipe is traditionally favored for the winter season. The original firepots burned charcoal. The heat from the brazier warmed guests on the outside, while the hot food warmed them on the inside.

1 whole chicken breast
½ lb. medium-sized prawns in the shell
½ lb. ground lean pork
2 green onions
2 stalks celery
1 package (about 1 lb.) firm bean cake
1 bunch (about l lb.) spinach
¼ head iceberg lettuce
11 c. (2 qt. plus 3 c.) chicken stock

Seasoning for Chicken:

½ tsp. salt
½ tsp. sugar

Seasoning for Pork:

½ tsp. salt
½ tsp. sugar
¾ tsp. thin soy sauce
dash of pepper
1 tsp. cornstarch

Dipping Sauce:

¼ c. thin soy sauce
2 tsp. sesame oil
⅛ tsp. pepper

Serves 4

NOODLES, WON TONS, AND RICE

DAN DAN NOODLES
(Dan Dan Mein)

½ lb. ground lean pork
¼ lb. barbecued pork or cooked ham
2 qt. water
1 lb. fresh Chinese noodles
3 tbsp. oil
⅓ c. chicken stock
1 c. shredded canned winter bamboo
  shoots
½ lb. bean sprouts
2 green onions, finely chopped

Seasoning:

¾ tsp. salt
¾ tsp. sugar
¾ tsp. thin soy sauce
2 tsp. cornstarch

Sauce:

1½ tbsp. bean sauce
1½ tbsp. chili paste with garlic
3 tbsp. oyster sauce
2 tsp. sugar

Serves 5

1. Place ground pork in a bowl. Add seasoning ingredients and mix well.
2. Cut barbecued pork or ham into thin strips, julienne style.
3. To make the sauce, mash bean sauce to a paste. Add chili paste, oyster sauce, and sugar and mix well.
4. Bring water to a boil in a wok or large saucepan. Add noodles and stir to prevent sticking. Boil, uncovered, for 2 minutes. Pour into colander and rinse under cold water. Drain.
5. Heat wok and add 1 tbsp. oil. Add ground pork and stir-fry for 2 minutes over high heat. Add chicken stock and bamboo shoots. Cover and cook for 2 minutes over high heat.
6. Add bean sprouts and barbecued pork. Stir-fry for 1 minute over high heat. Remove from wok and set aside.
7. Rinse and stir noodles under cold water. Drain; they must be slightly moist so they won't stick together when stir-fried. Immediately heat wok, add 2 tbsp. oil, and then the noodles. Stir-fry for 2 minutes over high heat.
8. Add sauce mixture and mix thoroughly. Then add pork mixture and mix well.
9. Remove to a platter and sprinkle with green onions. Serve.

Advance preparation: Steps 1–6 may be done a few hours in advance and kept at room temperature.

Variations: Use ground lean beef in place of the pork. Substitute 10 snow peas or 2 stalks celery for bamboo shoots. If using snow peas, remove tips and cut in half on the diagonal. If using celery, peel and cut into 1½″-long pieces; then lengthwise into strips, julienne style. Add snow peas or celery in step 6 with the bean sprouts.

CHICKEN TOPPING ON NOODLES
(Gai Kow Mein)

1. Skin and bone chicken. Cut into pieces 1½" by ½". Place in a bowl.
2. Add seasoning ingredients to chicken. Mix well.
3. Remove tips from snow peas. Cut in half on the diagonal.
4. Combine broth ingredients in a saucepan and bring to a boil. Keep hot.
5. Bring water to a boil in a wok or large saucepan. Add noodles and stir to prevent sticking. Boil, uncovered, for 3 minutes. Pour into colander. Rinse under cold running water. Drain.
6. Heat wok and add oil. Add chicken and stir-fry for 2 minutes over high heat.
7. Add chicken stock, soy sauce, mushrooms, and snow peas. Bring to a boil.
8. Stir in thickener. Cook for 30 seconds.
9. Add the noodles to hot broth and bring quickly to a boil. Transfer to a large serving bowl and spoon chicken mixture on top. Serve.

Advance preparation: Steps 1–7 may be done a few hours in advance and kept at room temperature.

1 whole chicken breast
25 snow peas
2 qt. water
1 lb. Chinese fresh noodles
1 tbsp. oil
½ c. chicken stock
1 tbsp. dark soy sauce
1 c. sliced mushrooms

Seasoning:

1 tsp. salt
1 tsp. sugar
1 tsp. thin soy sauce
1 tsp. white wine
1 tsp. oyster sauce
dash of pepper
1 tbsp. cornstarch
1 green onion, slivered

Broth:

6 c. chicken stock
2 tsp. dark soy sauce

Thickener:

1½ tbsp. cornstarch, mixed well with 3 tbsp. cold water

Serves 6–8

NOODLES IN GRAVY
(Yee Mein)

10 small Chinese dried black
  mushrooms, or ¼ lb. fresh
  mushrooms
¼ lb. barbecued pork
½ lb. bok choy
1 qt. water
1 package (8 oz.) deep-fried Chinese
  noodles
3 tbsp. oil
½ lb. bean sprouts
2 green onions, slivered
½ tsp. salt
½ tsp. sugar
2 tbsp. oyster sauce

Thickener:

2 tsp. cornstarch, mixed well with 1
  tbsp. cold water

Serves 6

1. Boil dried mushrooms in water to cover for 10 minutes. Drain, rinse, and squeeze dry. Remove and discard stems. Thinly slice caps. If using fresh mushrooms, thinly slice.
2. Cut barbecued pork into slices 1″ by ½″ by ¼″.
3. Break branches off center stalk of bok choy. Remove and discard any flowers. Peel tough skin off center stalk. Cut stalk and branches into 2″ pieces on the diagonal.
4. Bring water to a boil in a wok or large saucepan. Add noodles and stir a little to prevent the noodles from sticking. Boil, uncovered, for 3 minutes. Drain in colander and set aside.
5. Heat wok and add 1 tbsp. oil. Add bok choy, bean sprouts, green onions, barbecued pork, and mushrooms and stir-fry for 3 minutes over high heat, sprinkling with salt and sugar. Remove from wok and set aside.
6. Rinse and stir noodles under cold water. Drain; they must be slightly moist so they won't stick together when stir-fried. Immediately heat wok, add 2 tbsp. oil, and then the noodles. Stir-fry for 2 minutes over high heat.
7. Add vegetable mixture and oyster sauce. Mix well.
8. Stir in thickener. Cook for 30 seconds. Serve.

Advance preparation: Steps 1–6 may be done a few hours in advance and kept at room temperature.

NOODLES IN OYSTER SAUCE
(Gon Lo Mein)

1. In a wok or large saucepan, bring water to a boil. Add noodles and stir a little to prevent the noodles from sticking. Boil, uncovered, for 3 minutes. Remove from the heat, drain, pour into colander, rinse with cold water, and drain. If you are not using the noodles within 20 minutes, rinse them with cold water and drain again before stir-frying. They must be slightly moist when stir-fried or they will stick together.
2. Heat wok and add 2 tbsp. oil. Add noodles and stir-fry for 2 minutes over high heat.
3. Add sesame oil, oyster sauce, green onions, salt, and soy sauce. Mix well and serve.

Advance preparation: The noodles may be boiled a few hours in advance and kept at room temperature. Rinse and drain before stir-frying.

Serving suggestion: Serve for lunch with a garnish of sliced cooked ham or barbecued pork.

2 qt. water
1 lb. fresh Chinese noodles
2 tbsp. oil
1 tbsp. sesame oil
2 tbsp. oyster sauce
2 green onions, chopped
½ tsp. salt
2 tsp. thin soy sauce

Serves 5

PAN-FRIED NOODLES
(Jin Mein)

2½ qt. water
1 lb. fresh Chinese noodles
3 tbsp. oil
2 tsp. dark soy sauce
½ tsp. salt

1. In a wok or large saucepan, bring water to a boil. Divide noodles into 2 equal portions. Add 1 portion to water and stir to prevent sticking. Boil, uncovered, for 2 minutes.
2. While noodles are cooking, heat frying pan over high heat. (Frying pan must be quite hot so the noodles do not stick, but not hot enough to burn them. A frying pan with a nonstick coating is ideal.) Add 1½ tbsp. oil. Reduce heat to medium-high. With a Chinese wire strainer, remove noodles from boiling water. Allow them to drain slightly and then add them to the hot frying pan. Add 1 tsp. soy sauce and mix thoroughly. Flatten noodles to cover bottom of frying pan. Pan-fry until golden brown on the underside (about 5 minutes). Check bottom of pancake periodically to prevent burning.
3. Invert pancake. Sprinkle with ¼ tsp. salt and pan-fry until golden brown on second side (about 5 minutes). While still hot, break pancake into a bowl.
4. Repeat boiling and frying procedures with remaining noodles.

Advance preparation: Noodles may be pan-fried a few days in advance and refrigerated.

BEEF CHOW MEIN
(Ngow Yuk Chow Mein)

1. Prepare fried noodles.
2. Cut flank steak lengthwise (with grain of meat) into 3 equal strips each approximately 1½" wide. Cut each strip across the grain into thin slices. Place in a bowl.
3. Add seasoning ingredients to beef. Mix well.
4. Peel celery. Cut into 1½"-long pieces. Cut each piece lengthwise into strips, julienne style.
5. Heat wok and add 1 tbsp. oil. Add celery and bean sprouts and stir-fry for 2 minutes over high heat, sprinkling with salt and sugar. Remove from wok and set aside.
6. Heat wok and add 2 tbsp. oil. Add beef and stir-fry for 2 minutes over high heat.
7. Add chicken stock and bring to a boil.
8. Add vegetables, noodles, oyster sauce, and soy sauce. Stir-fry for 1 minute over medium heat. Serve.

Advance preparation: Steps 1–6 may be completed a few hours in advance and kept at room temperature.

Variation: Substitute chicken for the beef. Bone and skin 1 whole chicken breast and cut into strips 1½" by ½". Stir-fry for 2 minutes in step 6. In step 7, increase chicken stock to 1 c.; cover and cook for 2 minutes before proceeding to step 8.

Note: Leftover chow mein may be refrigerated for several days. Reheat in a microwave oven or stir-fry in a nonstick frying pan without oil for 2 minutes.

1 recipe Pan-Fried Noodles (preceding)
½ lb. flank steak
3 stalks celery
3 tbsp. oil
1 lb. bean sprouts
½ tsp. salt
½ tsp. sugar
¾ c. chicken stock
2 tbsp. oyster sauce
1 tsp. thin soy sauce

Seasoning:

½ tsp. salt
½ tsp. sugar
1 tsp. thin soy sauce
2 tsp. oyster sauce
1 tbsp. cornstarch

Serves 6

TOMATO BEEF CHOW MEIN
(Fon Kerr Ngow Yuk Chow Mein)

1 recipe Pan-fried Noodles (preceding)
½ lb. flank steak
2 stalks celery
½ medium-sized yellow onion
1 green bell pepper
3 medium-sized tomatoes
3 tbsp. oil
¼ tsp. salt
¼ tsp. sugar

Seasoning:

½ tsp. salt
½ tsp. sugar
1 tsp. thin soy sauce
1 tsp. oyster sauce
2 tsp. cornstarch

Sauce:

½ c. water
1½ tbsp. cider vinegar
2 tbsp. catsup
¼ tsp. salt
1 tsp. thin soy sauce
2 tbsp. sugar

Serves 8

1 . Prepare fried noodles.
2. Cut flank steak lengthwise (with grain of meat) into 3 equal strips each approximately 1½" wide. Cut each strip across the grain into thin slices. Place in a bowl.
3. Add seasoning ingredients to beef. Mix well.
4. Peel celery. Cut into 1½"-long pieces. Cut each piece lengthwise into strips, julienne style.
5. Cut yellow onion into wedges ¼" thick.
6. Cut bell pepper in half and remove and discard seeds. Cut into 1" squares.
7. Cut each tomato into 8 equal wedges.
8. Combine sauce ingredients and mix well.
9. Heat wok and add 1 tbsp. oil. Add celery, onion, and bell pepper and stir-fry for 2 minutes over high heat, sprinkling lightly with salt and sugar. Remove from wok and set aside.
10. Heat wok and add 2 tbsp. oil. Add beef and stir-fry for 2 minutes. Remove from wok and set aside.
11. Add sauce and tomatoes to wok and bring quickly to a boil. Add stir-fried meat and vegetables. Mix thoroughly and quickly return to a boil.
12. Add noodles. Mix and stir for 1 minute over medium heat. Serve.

Advance preparation: The sauce ingredients (step 8) may be combined a day ahead and kept at room temperature. Steps 1–7 and 9 and 10 may be completed a few hours in advance and kept at room temperature.

BASIC WON TONS
(Won Ton Haum)

1. Boil dried mushrooms in water to cover for 10 minutes. Drain, rinse, and squeeze dry. Remove and discard stems. Chop into very small pieces.
2. Shell, devein, wash, and drain prawns. Chop into very small pieces.
3. If using fresh water chestnuts, peel and remove and discard top and root ends. Finely chop fresh or canned water chestnuts.
4. Combine mushrooms, prawns, water chestnuts or jicama, pork, and green onion in a bowl.
5. Add seasoning ingredients to prawn mixture. Mix well.
6. See the accompanying diagram for instructions on folding won tons. Recipes using the won tons follow.

Advance preparation: Won tons may be formed a few hours in advance of cooking and kept at room temperature. They may also be frozen for up to 3 months. Freeze, well spaced, on a baking sheet, then transfer to an airtight container. They need not be defrosted before cooking (and should not be defrosted for more than 30 minutes).

10 small Chinese dried black mushrooms
1/4 lb. medium-sized prawns in the shell
5 fresh or 7 canned water chestnuts, or 2 tbsp. finely chopped jicama
1 1/4 lb. ground lean pork
1 green onion, finely chopped
1 package (1 lb.) won ton skins (about 80 skins)

Seasoning:

1 tsp. salt
1/2 tsp. sugar
2 tsp. thin soy sauce
1 tbsp. oyster sauce
dash of pepper
1 1/4 tbsp. cornstarch
1 small egg

Makes about 80

HOW TO WRAP A WON TON

1. With one corner of the skin toward you, place 1 tsp. filling about 1″ in from the corner.
2. Fold the corner nearest you over to cover the filling.
3. Fold from the same side once more, about 3/4″.
4. Turn the won ton 180 degrees so that the point of the triangle is toward you. Dampen the left corner with a little water.
5. Swing the right corner away from you and place it on top of the dampened left corner. As you make this fold, simultaneously pull the filling toward you with your middle finger. You should finish with a hatlike effect.

DEEP-FRIED WON TONS
(Jow Won Ton)

40 (½ recipe) Basic Won Tons
  (preceding)
2½ c. oil for deep-frying

Makes 40

1. Prepare the won tons.
2. Heat oil in wok to 325 degrees. Deep-fry won tons for 10 minutes, being careful not to add too many to the oil at once. Remove and drain on paper towels. Serve hot.

Advance preparation: The won tons can be fried a few hours in advance and kept at room temperature. Reheat for 8 minutes in a preheated 400-degree oven.

Serving suggestion: Fried won tons make excellent appetizers. Serve with Sweet-and-Sour Dipping Sauce (following).

SWEET-AND-SOUR DIPPING SAUCE

½ c. water
3 tbsp. cider vinegar
¼ c. sugar
1½ tbsp. catsup

Thickener:

1½ tbsp. cornstarch, mixed well with
  2 tbsp. water

Makes about ¾ c.

1. Combine water, vinegar, sugar, and catsup in a pan and bring to a boil, stirring to dissolve sugar.
2. Stir in thickener. Cook for 1 minute. Serve warm or at room temperature.

Advance preparation: This sauce can be made a few hours in advance and kept at room temperature. Reheat if desired.

WON TONS IN GRAVY

(Mun Yee Won Ton)

1. Prepare the won tons.
2. Heat oil in wok to 325 degrees. Deep-fry won tons for 10 minutes. Remove and drain on paper towels.
3. Cut barbecued pork or ham into ½" dice. Slice mushrooms.
4. Bring chicken stock to a boil in a wok or large saucepan. Add barbecued pork or ham, mushrooms, green onion, peas, and fried won tons. Cover and cook for 2 minutes over high heat.
5. Stir in the egg whites just until set. Immediately remove from the heat and serve.

Advance preparation: The won tons may be deep-fried several hours in advance and kept at room temperature.

Serving suggestion: Serve as a one-dish lunch or with Prawns with Chinese Long Beans and Steamed Rice for dinner.

40 (½ recipe) Basic Won Tons
  (preceding)
3 c. oil for deep-frying
2 oz. barbecued pork or cooked ham
¼ lb. fresh mushrooms
5 c. chicken stock
1 green onion, chopped
½ c. fresh or defrosted frozen peas
2 egg whites, lightly beaten

Thickener:

2½ tbsp. cornstarch, mixed well with
  ¼ c. water
1 tbsp. dark soy sauce
1 tbsp. sesame oil

Serves 4

WON TONS IN OYSTER SAUCE

(Ho Yau Gon Lo Won Ton)

1. Prepare the won tons.
2. In a wok or large saucepan, bring water to a boil. Add won tons and boil, uncovered, for 5 minutes. Stir occasionally while cooking.
3. Remove won tons with a Chinese wire strainer and drain in a colander.
4. Put the cooked won tons in a deep serving bowl. Add sesame oil and oyster sauce and mix carefully.
5. Garnish with green onion.

Note: If you have won tons in your freezer, this is a good recipe in which to use them.

40 (½ recipe) Basic Won Tons
  (preceding)
2 qt. water
1½ tbsp. sesame oil
3 tbsp. oyster sauce
1 green onion, chopped

Serves 4

WON TON SOUP
(Tong Won Ton)

40 (½ recipe) Basic Won Tons
   (preceding)
2 qt. water

Broth:

5 c. chicken stock
2 c. shredded Napa cabbage

Serves 4

1. Prepare the won tons.
2. To prepare the broth, bring chicken stock to a boil in a wok or large saucepan. Add Napa cabbage and cook for 2 minutes. Keep warm over low heat.
3. Meanwhile, bring water to a boil in another large pan. Add the won tons and cook, uncovered, for 5 minutes. Stir occasionally while cooking.
4. Remove the won tons from the boiling water with a Chinese wire strainer or drain in a colander. Place 10 won tons in each of 4 individual serving bowls. Ladle the hot broth over the won tons. Serve immediately.

Variations: Any leafy green vegetable may be used in place of the cabbage to add color and flavor to the broth. Thin slices of cooked meat, such as chicken, ham, or barbecued pork, may also be added.

STEAMED RICE
(Bok Fon)

1. Put rice in a heavy 2-qt. saucepan. Wash it thoroughly in 4 changes of cold water. Drain off water.
2. Add the 3 c. water to the rice, cover, and bring to a boil over high heat. This takes about 7–8 minutes.
3. Remove cover and continue cooking for about 5 minutes over high heat, or until the surface water is absorbed.
4. Re-cover, reduce heat to low, and cook for 5 minutes. The heat must be very low, as the rice scorches easily at this point. (If it should scorch, remove pot from heat. Place a slice of bread on the rice to absorb the burned flavor, re-cover, and let stand for 10 minutes. Discard the bread.) Fluff rice and serve.

Note: The Chinese have a practical way of measuring the amount of water needed to cook rice. To try this method, place the tip of your forefinger so that it barely touches the surface of the rice, then add water to cover the first joint. There will be about 1″ of water above the rice. When using an electric rice cooker, add water to about ¾″ above the level of the rice, or follow the manufacturer's instructions. If you are using one of the commercial "precooked" rices, follow the package directions.

It is advisable to use a 1-qt. saucepan when cooking 1 c. of raw rice, a 2-qt. saucepan for 2 c., and a 3-qt. saucepan for 3 c. Also, almost all Chinese cooks wash raw rice before cooking it and they *never* add salt to the pot.

2 c. long-grain white rice*
3 c. cold water

Plan on 1 c. raw rice yielding about 2½ c. cooked rice. Allow about 1 c. cooked rice per person. If you are serving Asians, double that amount. To reheat leftover rice, steam over boiling water until heated through, about 5 minutes, or place in a microwave oven for 2 minutes. Leftover rice may also be used to make Fried Rice (following).

Makes about 5 c.

FRIED RICE
(Chow Fon)

¼ lb. barbecued pork
¼ head iceberg lettuce
3½ tbsp. oil
3 eggs, lightly beaten
4 c. cold Steamed Rice (preceding)
1 green onion, finely chopped
¾ c. fresh or defrosted frozen peas
1 c. bean sprouts
1 tsp. salt
1 tbsp. oyster sauce
2 tsp. dark soy sauce

Serves 6

1. Cut barbecued pork into ½" cubes.
2. Finely shred lettuce. You should have about 1 c.
3. Heat wok and add 1 tbsp. oil. Add eggs and scramble until just set over medium-high heat. Remove from wok and set aside.
4. Heat wok and add 2½ tbsp. oil. Add rice and stir-fry for 3 minutes over medium heat. (If you are using rice that has been stored in the refrigerator and it is hard, add 2 tsp. water to soften it.) Be sure to stir constantly so that the rice does not burn.
5. Add barbecued pork, green onion, peas, and bean sprouts. Stir-fry for 2 minutes over high heat.
6. Add salt, oyster sauce, and soy sauce. Mix thoroughly.
7. Add shredded lettuce and scrambled eggs. Mix well. Serve.

Advance preparation: The steamed rice may be cooked a few days in advance and refrigerated. Steps 2 and 3 may be done a few hours in advance and kept at room temperature.

Variations: Use cubed cooked chicken, turkey, or ham or bay shrimp in place of the barbecued pork.

Note: Making a batch of fried rice is the equivalent of throwing together a pot of Mulligan's stew. Almost any leftover meat or vegetable can go into it.

SWEET RICE
(Gnaw Mai Fon)

1. Steam Chinese sausage for 15 minutes. Dice into small pieces. It is not necessary to steam the ham or barbecued pork. Simply dice it.
2. Put rice in a heavy 2-qt. saucepan. Wash thoroughly in 4 changes of water. Drain off water.
3. Add the 2 c. water, cover, and bring to a boil over high heat. This takes about 7–8 minutes.
4. Remove cover and continue cooking for about 5 minutes over high heat until the surface water is absorbed.
5. Re-cover, reduce heat to low, and cook for 5 minutes. The heat must be very low at this point, as the rice scorches easily. (If it should scorch, remove pot from heat. Place a slice of bread on the rice to absorb the burned flavor, re-cover, and let stand for 10 minutes. Discard the bread.)
6. Heat wok and add oil. Add sausage, ham, or barbecued pork, jicama or celery, and green onion and stir-fry for 1 minute over high heat.
7. Add cooked rice, salt, oyster sauce, and soy sauce. Mix thoroughly and serve.

Advance preparation: The entire recipe may be completed in advance and reheated by steaming over boiling water for 5 minutes, or until heated through, or by placing in a microwave oven for about 2 minutes.

Serving suggestion: Serve as a one-dish dinner or use as a stuffing for poultry.

2 *Chinese pork sausages, or* ¼ *lb. barbecued pork or cooked ham*
2 *c. sweet rice*
2 *c. cold water*
2 *tbsp. oil*
¾ *c. chopped jicama or celery*
1 *green onion, finely chopped*
½ *tsp. salt*
1 *tbsp. oyster sauce*
1½ *tsp. dark soy sauce*

Serves 6

INDEX

Abalone in oyster sauce 106
Appetizers
  Chinese doughnuts 36
  Chinese fried dumplings 39
  egg rolls 38
  parchment chicken 41
  pot stickers 43
  shrimp balls 45
  shrimp cakes 46
  shrimp toast 47
Asparagus
  with beef 90
  with chicken 68
  in oyster sauce 124
  with prawns 114

Barbecued pork, Chinese 94
Bean cake
  chow 125
  deep-fried 128
  steamed stuffed 127
  stuffed 126
  stuffed, in broth 127
Bean cake sauce chicken 69
Bean sprouts with mixed vegetables 125
Beef
  with asparagus 90
  chow mein 149
  tomato beef chow mein 150
  in clay pot 138
  Hunan 91
  Mongolian 92
  mo shu 79
  in oyster sauce 88
  for rice soup 50
  stew, Cantonese 89
  tomato 93
Black bean sauce
  clams 109
  prawns 113
  prawns, steamed 116
  spareribs 101
Bok choy with shrimp cake 117
Broccoli chicken 70

Cabbage, spiced 129
Cantonese
  beef stew 89
  boiled chicken 62

chicken salad 64
steamed chicken 84
steamed salmon 122
Cashew
  chicken 66
  prawns and scallops 107
Chicken
  with asparagus 68
  with bean cake sauce 69
  boiled, Cantonese 62
  with broccoli 70
  cashew 66
  chow mein 149
  in clay pot 139
  corn soup 52
  and cucumber 72
  curried 73
  garlic 74
  in hot bean sauce 67
  Hunan 75
  Jennie's pan-fried 76
  lemon 77
  meatball soup 53
  mo shu 79
  parchment 41
  pineapple 80
  pine nut 81
  for rice soup 51
  salad, Cantonese 64
  sesame 82
  steamed, Cantonese 84
  Szechuan spiced 85
  topping on noodles 145
  whiskey soup 54
  wings in soy sauce 83
Chinese
  barbecued pork 94
  doughnuts 36
  fried dumplings 38
  long beans with prawns 115
  sausage and pork cakes 98
Chow bean cake 125
Chow mein
  beef 149
  chicken 149
  tomato beef 150
Clams in black bean sauce 109

Clay pot
  beef 138
  chicken 139
  scallops and prawns 137
  spareribs 136
Cucumber
  with chicken 71
  and chicken salad 72
Curried
  chicken 73
  prawns 110

Dan dan noodles 144
Deep-fried
  bean cakes 128
  prawns 110
  won tons 152
Doughnuts, Chinese 36
Duck and potatoes 86
Dumplings, Chinese fried 38

Egg
  flower soup 55
  foo yung 134
Eggplant, spiced 129
Egg rolls 39

Firepot, Mongolian 141
Fish. *See* specific kinds
Fish in gravy, Jennie's 121
Foo yung, egg 134
Fried rice 156

Garlic chicken 74

Hoisin sauce spareribs 95
Hot-and-sour soup 56
Hot bean sauce chicken 67
Hot pepper toss 133
Hot spiced oil 44
Hunan
  beef 91
  chicken 75

Jennie's fish in gravy 121
Jennie's pan-fried chicken 76

Kohlrabi in Hunan sauce 130
Kung du pork 96
Kung pao scallops 119

Lemon chicken 77
Long beans with prawns, Chinese 115
Lotus root pork 99

Mandarin pancakes 78
Mixed vegetables with bean sprouts 125
Mongolian
    beef 92
    firepot 141
Mo shu chicken with mandarin pancakes 79
Mushrooms in oyster sauce 131
Mustard greens, pickled 132

Noodles
    with chicken topping 145
    dan dan 144
    in gravy 146
    in oyster sauce 147
    pan-fried 148

Oil, hot spiced 44
Oyster sauce
    asparagus 124
    abalone 106
    beef 88
    mushrooms 131
    noodles 147
    won tons 153

Pan-fried chicken, Jennie's 76
Pan-fried noodles 148
Parchment chicken 41
Pickled mustard greens 132
Pigs' feet in vinegar sauce 97
Pineapple chicken 80
Pine nut chicken 81
Pork
    Chinese barbecued 94
    and Chinese sausage cakes, steamed 98
    king du 96
    with lotus root 99
    meatballs for rice soup 51
    pigs' feet in vinegar sauce 97
    and shrimp filling for doughnuts 37
    spareribs in black bean sauce 101
    spareribs in clay pot 136
    spareribs in hoisin sauce 95
    with string beans 100
    sweet-and-sour 102
    twice-cooked 103

Potatoes and duck 86
Pot stickers 43
Prawns. *See* also shrimp
    with asparagus 114
    in black bean sauce 113
    and chicken sizzling platter 140
    with Chinese long beans 115
    curried 110
    deep-fried 110
    mo shu 79
    red pepper 111
    and scallops in clay pot 137
    and scallops in cashew nuts 107
    spiced 118
    steamed with black bean sauce 116
    a la Szechuan 112

Red pepper prawns 111
Rice
    fried 156
    soup 50
    soup, sizzling 58
    steamed 155
    sweet 157

Salad
    Cantonese chicken 64
Salmon, Cantonese steamed 122
Sand dabs, steamed 122
Scallops
    kung pao 119
    and prawns in clay pot 137
    and prawns with cashew nuts 107
Seaweed soup 57
Sesame chicken 82
Shrimp
    balls 45
    cakes 46
    cakes with bok choy 117
    spiced 118
    toast 47
Sizzling platter, chicken and prawn 140
Sizzling rice soup 58
Snow peas with squid 120
Soups
    basic rice 50
    chicken corn 52
    chicken meatball 53

chicken whiskey 54
egg flower 55
hot-and-sour 56
seaweed 57
sizzling rice 58
winter melon 59
won ton 154
Soy sauce chicken wings 83
Spareribs
    in black bean sauce 101
    in clay pot 136
    hoisin sauce 95
Spiced
    cabbage 129
    chicken, Szechuan 85
    eggplant 129
    prawns 118
Steamed
    chicken, Cantonese 84
    pork and Chinese sausage cakes 98
    prawns with black bean sauce 116
    rice 155
    salmon, Cantonese 122
    stuffed bean cake 127
    sweet rice 157
Stew, Cantonese beef 89
Sweet-and-sour pork 102
Sweet filling for doughnuts 37
Sweet rice 157
Szechuan
    prawns 112
    spiced chicken 85

Taro basket 108
Tomato
    beef 93
    beef chow mein 150
Twice-cooked pork 103

Winter melon soup 59
Won tons
    basic 151
    deep-fried 152
    in gravy 153
    in oyster sauce 153
    soup 154